My *BRILLIANT CAREER*

MY *BRILLIANT CAREER*

12 HIGH ACHIEVERS REVEAL
THE SECRETS OF THEIR SUCCESS

JEFF GROUT & LYNNE CURRY

KOGAN PAGE

First published in 2000

Kogan Page Limited
120 Pentonville Road
London
N1 9JN
UK

Kogan Page Limited
163 Central Avenue, Suite 2
Dover
NH 03820
USA

British Library Cataloguing in Publication Data

A CIP record for this book is available from the British Library.

ISBN 0 7494 3361 2

Typeset by Jean Cussons Typesetting, Diss, Norfolk
Printed and bound by Creative Print and Design (Wales) Ebbw Vale

Contents

About the authors

Jeff Grout is the European corporate development director of Robert Half International (RHI), the world's largest specialist recruitment consultancy. Over more than 20 years, as RHI's UK managing director, he accumulated a wealth of knowledge on the imperfect science of achieving a brilliant career. He also steered the company from an operation with two offices and 12 staff into a business with a domestic turnover of £63 million, 19 offices and more than 320 staff. He is a frequent commentator and columnist in his field, has collaborated with the BBC in producing an interview training video, and run interview technique courses for companies including Marks & Spencer, Lloyds Bank, British Airways and Merrill Lynch.

Lynne Curry is a freelance writer with a background in newspapers in the provinces and in London.

My Brilliant Career is their second collaboration. The first, *The Adventure Capitalists*, is also published by Kogan Page.

About the subjects

Ken Bates

Ken Bates is a successful entrepreneur whose career has spanned road haulage, ready-made concrete, buying one of the British Virgin Islands and setting up the Irish Trust Bank. But he is best known for achieving the dream of many: he owns his own football club, Chelsea FC, which he bought for £1 in 1982, when the club was in the second division and the ground described as 'a ramshackle bowl'. He is now chairman and the club is in the Premier League. He has been described by the former MP and football commentator (and Chelsea fan) David Mellor as 'more ruthless than Saddam Hussein'.

Roger Black

Roger Black represented Britain at the highest level for 14 years as a 400-metres runner and member of the 4 × 400-metres relay team. He won 15 major European championship medals – but his greatest achievement was winning the Olympic 400-metres silver medal in 1996. He abandoned a degree in medicine at Southampton University to concentrate on athletics and now uses his experience of transforming dreams and goals into reality as a motivational speaker. He is also a presenter for BBC television sport. He was awarded the MBE in 1992.

Raymond Blanc

Raymond Blanc arrived in England in 1972, to become one of the first culinary superstars in the UK and probably the best-known Frenchman in England. His restaurant and country house hotel, Le Manoir aux Quat'Saisons, Oxfordshire, was one of the first to awake the British interest in food, and has remained acclaimed while others have come and gone. Blanc is also a successful author and broadcaster – and he has trained many other chefs who are today Michelin stars who have gone on to huge success. Le Manoir aux Quat'Saisons stands now as one of the great centres of culinary excellence and one of the most beautiful places in Europe. He remains passionate about cooking and ingredients and has been a member of the Soil Association, the organic farming and food certification body, for nearly 20 years.

Sir Chay Blyth

Sir Chay Blyth, a former soldier in the Parachute Regiment, became the first man to sail around the world against the prevailing winds and currents – described as 'the most outstanding passage ever made by one man alone'. He went on to turn yacht racing into a successful business, organizing and raising sponsorship for high-profile sailing challenges, including the BT Global Challenge, which invites amateur sailors to pay more than £20,000 for 'a massive culture shock' and the adventure of their lives, and which is fully booked until the year 2004. More than 30 years ago, Blyth broke the record for rowing across the Atlantic with Army captain John Ridgeway (3,000 miles in 92 days).

Tony Bullimore

Tony Bullimore, a born entrepreneur, has had a successful career as a businessman, but it is as a yachtsman that he became known all over the world. Having safely raced over the Atlantic 30 times, having won 150 trophies and having been named as the Yachtsman of the Year, he found himself upside down – literally – in the freezing Southern Ocean when the keel of his boat snapped during one of the most challenging races in the world, the Vendée Globe. Tossed by gigantic waves, he survived for five days in an air pocket in the hull, amazing the world – which had seen TV pictures of the boat – by emerging alive and barely the worse for the ordeal. His survival was the apogee of the single-minded determination that has underlined his career.

Sebastian Coe (Lord Coe)

Sebastian Coe, ennobled in spring 2000, is one of the greatest sportsmen of the 20th century and a household name for his achievements on the running track. Twice Olympic 1500 metres champion, he once held the 800 metres, 1000 metres, 1500 metres and one-mile records simultaneously. His 800-metre world record endured for 16 years. After retiring from competitive athletics, he went into politics, becoming Conservative MP for Falmouth and Camborne in Cornwall – losing his seat in the New Labour landslide five years later in 1997. He was appointed Private Secretary to the Leader of the Opposition, William Hague, in the summer of 1997.

Harvey Goldsmith

Harvey Goldsmith has spent nearly 30 years at the top of his trade – a particular achievement in the risky business of music promotion. He was the promoter behind the rock world's first public display of concern for the developing world when a series of concerts was organized to raise funds for Cambodia. Eight years later, in 1886, he pulled together the celebrated Live Aid concert event in 10 weeks, bringing more artists on to one stage than ever before. Later, he moved away from pop and staged Pavarotti in the Park, the great tenor Luciano Pavarotti singing in Hyde Park before thousands of people. In a precarious milieu, he has had downs as well as ups and in 1999, after the failure of his Total Eclipse festival in Cornwall, he saw his company wound up. But Goldsmith, who has raised a quarter of a billion pounds for charity, was soon back in the fray.

Nicola Horlick

Nicola Horlick is a highly successful fund manager. But she became a nationally known face when her bank, which suspected she was about to leave with her team, suspended her. Denying this vehemently – a stance that she has continued to take – she responded by flying to the bank's headquarters in Frankfurt, with the media in tow, to demand her job back. Educated at Cheltenham Ladies College, she graduated in jurisprudence from Oxford and joined Warburg as a trainee in 1983, working there for eight years on what would become Mercury Asset Management. Most recently, she launched from scratch a new fund for Société Général: SG Asset Management. A mother of six, she lost her eldest daughter to leukaemia.

Michael Lynagh

Michael Lynagh is one of the modern greats of Rugby Union and Australia's greatest ever fly-half. He played 72 times for his country and scored 911 points, until recently the highest number of points scored in international rugby. Originally intent on playing cricket, he won a place in his school first XV at the age of 14, the launch pad of a brilliant career for Queensland University, Benetton Treviso in Italy and Saracens in London (he names Hampstead and Treviso as his homes, along with Sunshine Beach in Australia). He played for Australia in the first three rugby World Cups and was vice-captain of the Wallabies when they won the event in 1991. He captained the side for three years until he retired from the international game in 1995.

Michael Parkinson

Michael Parkinson is the consummate chat show host. Some of his interviews have become classic TV and it is a claim barely disputed that he has never been bettered. He returned to the screen in 1998 after a 16-year absence. Despite being made media personality of the year, Parkinson hates the idea of superstar journalists and interviewers who regard themselves as the subject of the exchange. The interview, he says, is 'basically an unnatural act performed by two consenting adults in public'. Parkinson, who began life as a local newspaper journalist, remains a sports columnist and is also an author and radio presenter. After National Service during which he became an Army captain, he worked for a series of national newspapers before moving to TV current affairs, presenting and producing programmes for Granada Television.

Tony Robinson

Tony Robinson is the actor who brought the character of Baldrick to life in the classic and much-admired *Blackadder* series. He is also a writer, director and presenter who has written more than a dozen children's books and presented many 'popular academic' series, such as the TV archaeology programme *Time Team*. He played the Sheriff of Nottingham in his own subversive production of *Maid Marian and her Merry Men*. He has been vice-president of the actors' union, Equity, and was one of the prominent show-business supporters of New Labour. Despite his youthful looks (and attitude) he has been performing on the stage for more than 40 years. Recently he was elected to the National Executive Committee of the Labour Party.

Robin Smith

Robin Smith is one of the greatest batsmen in English cricketing history – although he is South African. He came to England to join his brother, Chris (also a cricketer) for a month – and stayed. Captain of Hampshire, he scored 1,333 runs against the fearsome bowlers of the West Indies in 19 Tests. Having won 62 caps and played in 74 one-day internationals, with a Test average of 44, he was voted the second-most admired cricketer ever in *Cricketer's Who's Who*.

Introduction

Millions of people have brilliant careers but few become the most brilliant in their field. To aim for this apogee is understandable, but to expect to attain it is unrealistic for all but a handful.

The Robert Half Interview series set out to persuade members of that élite handful to share the secrets of their success. Were they lucky? Were they well connected? Were they born brilliant?

Over six years, more than 25 hugely successful people – with Sir Terence Conran as the first – have been asked by Jeff Grout what makes them different from the 'run-of the-mill'. They have talked frankly of the struggle to start, the determination to continue and the pleasure (and pain) of making it.

My Brilliant Career features 12 of these people, some of the most prominent luminaries of sport, business and the media. It examines the different constituent parts of a brilliant career: the natural flair, the desire to do the job, the determination often needed, and the hard work that every successful career involves. It looks at the influence of home and heroes, how much other people have contributed, what can be learnt from disaster and whether the rewards of a brilliant career are seen as mostly financial.

Robert Half International pioneered specialized staffing services in 1948 and today is the industry leader worldwide, with offices in North America, Europe and Australia. The interviews were conducted before audiences of senior business managers (more of whom wished to attend than could be accommodated) and it is hoped that their own careers benefited in a big or small way from what our brilliant subjects had to say.

1

Some are born great – the innate qualities that predispose success

Sorry. It was not an act of will that gifted Roger Black his ability to run. It was, if you like, an act of God, a whim of Nature, a happy collision of genes, the sheer luck of the congenital draw.

One summer's evening at the Southampton Athletics Club, with a year to kill while he re-sat his A levels and an ambition to follow his father into medicine, Black turned up for a training session. He had never trained before. His background was that of a good school athlete, but it was his shoes that struck Kriss Akabusi, already a recognized international athlete, clad from head to foot in the gear of his sponsors, Adidas.

Black arrived in 'a huge pair of canvas shoes which looked like boats' and, rather than a logo-spattered tracksuit top, he was wearing an old sweater. Then he leapt over his first hurdle and Akabusi instantly dismissed his sartorial shortcomings. This 'gangly, spotty, well-spoken youth' took the hurdles like a natural. More than 10 years later, Akabusi recalled his reaction in the *Independent on Sunday*:

> I remember watching the incredible ease with which Roger bounded over hurdles and thinking, 'Gosh, he's strong.' He'd just finished his A levels and was a very good junior English schools athlete, but had never trained before. Most athletes turn up for coaching all ready to go

– I was sponsored by Adidas and Todd [Bennett] by Nike, so we had matching uniforms with logos down to our socks. Not Roger. By January 1985 it was clear that we had a talent here...even though I was the recognized international athlete, it was easy to see that he was better than I was – he had pure speed and aggression. There was a sense of joy and anticipation in seeing what he was capable of.

Sorry? Yes: with his natural speed and strength, Black illustrates the inescapable truth about some brilliant careers – no amount of endeavour can make up for the intrinsic flair and talent on which they are founded. As sports feature writer Kate Battersby wrote in the *Evening Standard*: 'It looks horribly as if Black is one of the golden people who is brilliant at everything, although he claims to be "crap" at golf.'

Michael Lynagh, the brilliant Australian rugby player, was chosen for the first XV at his school when he was 14. He was fast, he could handle the ball, and he could visualize the right moves. These were abilities he simply had. A great coach nurtured and directed his talent at schoolboy level, and he never looked back, but Lynagh – an amazingly self-effacing man – has to confess that he was blessed with 'a lot of natural talent'.

If sport and athletics require a lucky birth – bringing with it such gifts as hand-to-eye coordination, ball skills, balance and build – many other brilliant careers begin on foundations much less galactic. Indeed, even Roger Black's talent came with a sting: a congenital heart problem discovered when he was 11, which required check-ups every two months and which prevented him doing any competitive sport for the first year (he is still monitored annually). Fortunately, he was also blessed with the ability to decide on a course of action and to stick to it. 'I've always had an attitude of trying not to complain, of just getting on with things, because the reality is that it could all end tomorrow,' Black told Nick Morgan of *The Guardian* in 1988.

That attitude – inherent or acquired – has been important to Black. As we will explore, running like the wind may be a prerequisite for success for a brilliant 400-metre competitor, but brilliance in other fields begins with other innate qualities that are less elusive and, thank goodness, rather more common. Is there a disposition that promises success? This chapter examines what our subjects have to say (and what they do not say) about their own characters.

Enthusiasm: the *sine qua non* of all achievement

You won't find enthusiasm in many books on success but it is, without doubt, the cornerstone of achievement. Each one of our subjects has it without exception, and without a doubt, there is no professional brilliance without it, even with a wealth of natural talent.

Enthusiasm may be called 'positivity' in management jargon but it amounts to the same thing. Here is Nicola Horlick on the quality she found she had at an early age, and that, above all else, she seeks in others. Asked what attributes she felt had contributed to her success, she replied:

> Enthusiasm is a pretty major one. It drives me insane that so many English people are so negative about things. Being positive is very important. I went to school in the States for a while on an exchange scholarship. I was completely amazed, I was suddenly surrounded by lots of people like me, who were all very positive and enthusiastic, and all the cynicism and negativity you get in the UK was left behind me, and I loved it. I wouldn't want to live in America – I don't really like the culture, but I loved that aspect of it. It's important that people have a positive attitude in life; it's nothing to do with succeeding, it's to do with getting the most out of life.

Enthusiasm, says Horlick, is the very plank of her success. 'I'm not sure that I'm driven, as such,' she says.

> I am enthusiastic. I am not consumed with the desire to be successful. People who write articles in newspapers think me and people like me sit down and think they're going to do this that and the other. Life

doesn't work like that. How do you know if you're going to be successful or not?

As a quality, enthusiasm is hard to beat. Prue Leith, the restaurateur and business woman, and a previous interviewee in the Robert Half Interview series, memorably dismissed the current fashion for detachment: 'I hate the laid back,' she declared (and yes, she thinks enthusiasm was a big part of her own success).

As an on-screen performer, Michael Parkinson might appear the epitome of the laid back. Lurking behind this appearance are great reserves of enthusiasm. More than 25 years after he first became famous through the *Parkinson* show, it shines through his dialogue. It also propelled him through a poor set of examination results, despite having won a place at Barnsley Grammar School. He left school with two O levels – no great achievement even in those less competitive days – but as he says, 'it didn't matter because I knew what I wanted to be. I wanted to be a journalist, the man who came round to our house every Monday morning on a Raleigh bicycle to get the cricket scores.'

True to his ambition, which was more wholehearted than lofty (for local newspaper sports reporters did not live the glamorous lives immortalized by black-and-white movies), he got the bike clips and he got the bike, and he rode around a 'nest' of pit villages for three years – and he was good at it. For Parkinson had another talent: fluency with words.

The ability to write can be a thorny subject. Successful and acclaimed novelists (Ian McEwan springs to mind) have come out of creative writing courses at universities, but Parkinson maintains that writing skills are a gift, not a learned craft.

I could always write. Doing television is easy by comparison. I can tell you how and why I do television … I can't tell you how to write. I haven't got a clue what happens. I sit down every Friday, I haven't got a thought in my head, and three hours or four hours later, I've got 1,500 words there. I don't know how it happens. I distrust people who say there is a writing course you can go on. I think writing is a gift; you can either write or you can't. I read an obituary today from a book in my bookcase – *200 years of the Observer*. I took it out and I had forgotten that I had written an obituary of Robert Morley when he died six or seven years ago. I read it and it was as if I was reading somebody else's work. I'd not only totally forgotten it but I couldn't imagine how I'd written that piece. I'd forgotten the anecdotes ... it was like reading somebody else's work. It was very strange and very odd. I think any writer will tell you that.

Even so, enthusiasm – and the curiosity bred of enthusiasm – have got Parkinson out of bed every morning with a light heart. His subjects have never bored him. One of the great privileges of his job, he says, has been to sit opposite great conversationalists. Jonathan Miller, Peter Ustinov, Gore Vidal and Jacob Bronowski are four he plucks from the archive:

You pick their brains and you think, 'This is like doing a university course in 90 minutes.' I did an interview with Bronowski that lasted an hour and 20 minutes and the *Listener* reprinted the entire interview in one edition. All they did was take my questions out and it read as prose. That was his genius. Every time you asked him a question, you were aware that the sentence he answered with was perfect in construction, in thought, in everything. It was like interviewing a Swiss watch. That kind of privilege is extraordinary.

Parkinson's huge relish emerges in his stories: Robert Mitchum, high on dope and answering every question 'yep' or 'nope'; Lee Marvin accompanying Parkinson into a bar in Soho where the landlady was a great fan, and demonstrating the scene from *Cat Ballou* where he pulls his gun out and his trousers fall down. Middle age has rounded Parkinson's perceptions and, if anything, swelled that bank of enthusiasm that enables him to enjoy his work.

My favourite class of people, if you like, would be old people, because they don't give a damn about what they say, which is a talk show host's dream. Dame Edith Evans was wonderful. 'Oh, he's a drunk,' she'd say, 'he groped me once.' She was bright and funny and glamorous in an old-fashioned sense. She would arrive in a white Rolls Royce at the BBC, with a fur coat on – no PC with Dame Edith – jewellery and a new frock by Norman Hartnell. She would storm in, no other word for it. We had a doorman called Alf, a one-armed pensioner, and she would go straight up to him and say, 'I was in the post office getting my pension and I said to the lady, "this is not enough, this is not good enough".' She would have this big talk with Alf about how the government must go, all that sort of thing.

The third time she did this, I dared to challenge her. You had to be careful with her – she was regal. I said to her, 'Dame Edith, don't you think it's a bit odd that you arrive at the BBC with the white mink on, the Norman Hartnell frock and the jewels and talk to Alf about the state of the old-age pension?' 'What's wrong with that?' she said. 'Also,' I went on, 'you arrive in a white Rolls Royce.' 'Would you have me arrive in a Mini?' she replied. I thought no, I wouldn't have her arrive in a Mini. She was a star, and she fulfilled the public's expectations of what a star should be like.

One of Parkinson's greatest talents, in fact, has been to appear so effortlessly talented – the very phrase used by Brian Reade, writing in *The Mirror* in 1998, when the *Parkinson* show returned to TV after a 16-year absence: 'Show me a man over 40 who has never envied Michael Parkinson and I'll show you a born liar,' Reade wrote. 'He is one of those effortlessly talented men, like Des Lynam, who takes lavish praise from peers and public in his stride, and maintains a street cred in a profession where smarminess and success go hand in hand.'

Is that the case? In fact, Parkinson has polished and honed those apparently effortless talents – a feature he shares with the examples of all our brilliant careerists. But being Parkinson has become something of a career in itself. 'I temporarily retired when I was 50, then 55, then 60,' he says. 'Now I've realized I'll never retire as long as I can hold a pen. I took time off a few years back and discovered the great truth that golf is not a way of life.'

Sir Chay Blyth is so convinced of the need for enthusiasm that he lists it at the top of his requirements to enlist for his BT round-the-world challenges. These events, in which teams of amateur sailors stake their savings and their necks, turn on pure passion. In Sir Chay's words:

> [The challenge] is about people seeing beyond their natural horizons. It is about the spirit that makes someone ignore seasickness and lack of sleep, pull on a damp set of thermals and struggle on deck at 3 am to make a sail change. That says more about you than any status symbol. To recycle a favourite phrase of mine: no guts, no glory.

He might have added: 'No enthusiasm, no chance.' He interviews potential participants for more than an hour. 'I look for one key ingredient: enthusiasm for the project,' he says. 'If they're not enthusiastic about it, or a bit mediocre, then forget it. It's not for them. Somewhere along the line they'll probably drop out and all they've done is waste their time and our time. It's not the money, it's enthusiasm.'

Curiosity: lethal only for cats

If enthusiasm is the bedrock of success, curiosity and a deficit of boredom are the foundations to which enthusiasm give rise.

By nature, Raymond Blanc is an epicurean, a lover of fine and beautiful things. His mother's cooking gave him a love of food, but it was a scene in his home city that inspired him to use food as part of a bigger picture.

It was an August night in Besançon that he discovered the talent that would give so much joy to so many people.

> When I saw the floodlit terrace of the restaurant in the full summer night I stopped and stared. The scene was stunning. Here was life at its best. Elegant guests holding hands and enjoying the food, the beautiful long lace cloths, the glittering silver and the fine china and oh… the fat chicken studded with black truffles and surrounded with a ballet of fresh water crayfish; the flambéing of the seabass, the carving of the cheese, the elegant and precise movements of the *maitre d'hotel*. The most beautiful spectacle I have ever seen. That night, I decided to be a chef.

Straight away ... from the first day, I educated my sense of smell on the wine glasses returned by the guests; I started to read everything about food, food chemistry first, food love, food sex, food history, food religion, food politics, food family, etc. I started to cook for my friends and would submerge into the huge beautiful history of food and wine.

Blanc's career as a commis chef in France came to an abrupt halt when he had a contretemps with the head chef, who hospitalized him by hurling an enormous copper pan. As he lay in the ward, his boss visited him and offered to help him obtain a work permit for England. Blanc was now convinced that his future lay in food. 'I strongly believe that every one of us has a talent and if we are curious enough we will find it, we will do so through trial and errors,' Blanc says.

I loved the idea of giving, and knew I had to be in an industry or somewhere that I could give and share something with people. I could not have been part of a factory. Before I found what I wanted to do, I was sent through the best engineering college but moved away because rational thought and logic (of which I had neither) were the basis of this particular learning. I believe there is no greater affliction in life than mediocrity and was desperate to find my niche. To become a nurse became the obvious choice – not just a nurse, a super nurse, at least Mother Teresa! Well that did not work either; the Catholic sisters in charge disapproved strongly of my friendliness towards the female nurses. Besides, I was working in a leukaemia department and could not handle the emotional baggage. For a little while, I worked in a factory and found it the darkest and the least inspiring place I have ever worked in and that little restaurant in Besançon became the focal point of my life.

According to Blanc, a fine chef needs imagination and to have imagination, he or she needs to possess curiosity, which will lead to discovery. It is very important never to accept what has been put in front of us.

Curiosity leads to imagination, leads to discovery. It is very important never to accept what has been put in front of you. Don't be a result of your own education. Think beyond, have the ability to constantly review and reinvent yourself, because we are in a world that is moving so fast. You have to be a bit of a workaholic as well, terribly passionate, don't work for money. Money will come by. If you are totally passionate, totally devoted to what you are doing and full of passion and enthusiasm, the commercial bit will come automatically.

Tony Robinson, the alter-ego of Baldrick, of the classic *Blackadder* TV series, and also a writer of children's books and presenter of more serious TV and radio programmes, says he was born curious and wanting to know everything about everything.

I am blotting paper really. Wherever I go, I suck up everything – everything – I really am a Hoover. I think that's one of the reasons why I've been able to do such a variety of different things; I am just interested in stuff. Maybe one of the results of not going to university is that I really am just so interested in everything. Never having really been able to learn, I just want to learn. If you've got something I don't know about, tell me, give it to me. I never speak much if I go to dinner parties. I always want to know what the other people are doing because soon they'll go and I won't know unless I ask now.

Robinson has an interesting take on what else might have marked him out from birth for his theatrical career: on the TV screen, if not in real life, he looks 'cute'!

Dirk Bogarde once said, 'I see myself on the television and when I open my eyes they go all watery and sexy and heterosexual and yet I'm the opposite of all that. That's what the screen does to me.' I think the same is true of me, in that I do look cute on television. I'm a bit of a bastard. In real life, a manipulative bastard, I'm power mad, paranoid, and all those other qualities that tend to help people get on the television – but I've got a pair of big eyes, and that's just part of my genetic make up.

An only child, Robinson had one foot in the world of fantasy when he was tiny. He lived, he says, 'completely' in a fantasy world, and 'lied all the time'.

You'd think that if a child was a performer he would be doing something that was so interesting that the rest of the time he could really afford to be very understated. But I always had to fantasize about who I was and what I was doing. I look back on it now and I can see this child doing it. It doesn't seem like me, it's like I can see a movie of this little child. I think of myself (and it's quite touching) as a poor little messed-up thing. On the other hand, it was good training for me as a writer and as a performer. I find it extraordinarily easily to devise story, to create narrative. If I'm with kids now, I just sit down and talk twaddle for half and hour, but it will be narrative twaddle, there will be characters in it and it will all come out happy in the end!

Harvey Goldsmith's first career choice (bearing no resemblance to the career he eventually pursued) was prompted by curiosity. What was it? Pharmacy! He was fascinated by the power of marketing, and how women could be swayed into buying products by the sheer power of an advertising campaign. His course included a year's apprenticeship in a pharmacy, and he decided to do that first.

Working in a chemist's shop, watching women coming in and choosing cosmetics, lipsticks and perfumes and toilet water, I could never figure out why they would choose one particular product over another. At the time, I would say that 80 to 90 per cent of women hadn't got a clue how cosmetics and perfume reacted with their skin. If they were told this was the smell, they would test it – they couldn't work out when they put it on to their body, or skin, that it would change, of if they tried a lipstick of a certain colour that it would change colour when they put it on their lips. I was fascinated by the branding of goods. You could always tell when there was some kind of advertising campaign going on because there would be a rush of people for products like Estée Lauder, or whatever product, and they wouldn't have a clue why they were buying it, they just knew they had to have it.

Energy: no carbohydrates necessary

It is sad for those of us of a more lethargic persuasion, but great success is often accompanied by great energy. It may not be the

Margaret Thatcher syndrome – four hours' sleep a night – but there is an element of unforced vigour in successful people. If not physical, it is mental. Usually, however, one predisposes the other. Tony Bullimore, whose worldwide fame sprung from surviving for five days in the upturned hull of his boat in the freezing ocean (a feat of mind in itself), appears almost frightened of missing something. What? He doesn't know. What he does know is that his mind is rarely in neutral. His faith in the power of his mind extends to a belief that many illnesses can be controlled by determination, and he cannot see himself ever retiring ('the word isn't in my vocabulary').

> Life to me is 24 hours a day, seven days a week – that's the part that's sad for my wife. My commitment to my projects is 24 hours. I wake up in the night and I have things clicking around and I go downstairs, have a cup of coffee, and I'm off with a notepad, writing things down. I have a never-ending supply of energy and a tremendous inbuilt ability to look after my body and mind. My nature is just simply to go for it. I've got projects I'll be doing after my catamaran trip round the world, a couple of things burning away on the back burner of my mind. I'm just that type of person.

Even in childhood, Bullimore was getting involved in various adventures and challenges. He came to realize that he was naturally a risk taker (although taking risks can be a conscious decision) and that left to his own devices, he would always go to the limits. 'I know the odd person who is similar to me,' he says. 'I have got involved in incredible risk, but that's the way it is. You win a few and you lose a few.' Bullimore lists his own strengths as determination and identifying opportunity.

> I have my own motto: nothing is impossible and nothing is impregnable. Determination is important with anything one does, and I have grit. I won't give up in any situation. Sometimes I actually need people to say, 'Let's drop it and move on to something else.'

Nicola Horlick, with a demanding job and five children, when asked how much time she got for herself, replies: 'Well, none of course.

Does that matter? It's not going to kill me, is it? I'm not the relaxing type, which is probably fortunate.'

Chay Blyth cannot envisage himself ever retiring or taking life easy. 'I don't think I'll ever retire. I'll just move on to other projects,' he says. After so many epic voyages, he never finds the sea dull or tame.

> I was out today on our new boat for the first time and I thought it was really great. The skipper is there to play with the boat, and look after its safety. My job is to deal and interact with the people on board. At the end of the day, business is about relationships, no matter what. My job is not to sail but to develop these relationships and to see what business we can do with these companies. I haven't got time to be bored; I'm trying to focus on getting these contracts.

Blind faith: dedication to a project

After nearly 30 years of promoting artists and staging concerts, it would be understandable if Harvey Goldsmith had had enough. Indeed, he is 'saddened,' he says, by the profit motive that drives the entertainment industry today. But he is still in touch with the excitement that first led him to abandon a career in pharmacy and wade into the tempestuous (and uncharted) waters of show business with all its risks. To be successful in business, Goldsmith says, there has to be commitment to the job in hand. Otherwise, it will fail. Persistence (which we look at next) comes a close second. He also possessed, although he did not initially appreciate it, innate organizational ability and an eye for talent.

> The first thing in starting out in business is that you have to believe in what you're doing. The second is don't take 'no' for an answer. The third is never look at the sky; look at the downside, because the blue skies are always there, but you must calculate your risks, because if the risk factors are right, the rewards will be there. They may not be as high as you expected, but a reward is a reward.

Goldsmith laments the changes in the business – driven, he says, by shortsightedness through the quest for instant rewards and profits. Nevertheless, he remains a man who still gets a buzz from the discovery of something new in his business, despite having done so on many occasions. 'Every time you see something that is raw talent, a new act or a new record, or something on television, it gives you the buzz to keep going,' he says. Cirque du Soleil, an original Canadian circus, and Club Tropicana, which had never been out of Cuba since its inception in 1939, have been among his recent finds.

What gets me up in the morning is the opportunity to break new barriers, find new talent, look for new forms of entertainment – and a son who's growing up fast. I enjoy it. The business has changed dramatically. In the early days you'd literally wake up in the morning and say, 'What are we going to do today, and how does it work?' Today, it's unfortunately too business orientated and not enough creative orientated. I believe we're suffering in the style of music around. Business has a grip on entertainment because, basically, you're dealing in the main with naive people who have come up. The razzmatazz of showbiz is that it doesn't matter who you are, what your background is, and where you come from – if you've got an innate talent, some creative juice or a message to put across through music and entertainment, it doesn't matter, it's open to you. It's a very hard pathway, but if you can succeed in it, the sky's the limit.

Goldsmith fails to mention, in his modesty, that there is a large chunk of personal charm involved in becoming a successful fixer, especially in the ego-infested seas of show business. At university, where he spent his time building up an entertainment organization that spanned the academic institutions of the south coast, he became friends with many of the artists he was putting on. He was asked to manage several. He still has charm and an accommodating manner, apparently without effort.

Tony Robinson tells hilarious tales of the compulsive-anarchistic nature of the set of *Blackadder*. The cast, he says, was all 'perfectionist manic-depressives'. Every week, the script would arrive and instead of starting rehearsals, the cast (all writers) would try to improve it.

When outside actors came in, they would be desperate with fear, never having had a proper rehearsal.

> We would say, 'This joke isn't funny, this joke isn't funny!' and come up with various formulations of the joke until eventually somebody would come up with the right formulation. We wouldn't laugh, we'd just go 'Yes! That's great! We've solved that problem, where's the next problem?' For a show like that, you rehearse it for about five days and then you go into a studio. A studio audience is invited in. By this time we'd forgotten that it was funny, we'd lost all confidence in it, so each week, when we got half way through the first scene and the laughs came, a little glint would pass between all our eyes which said 'phew, we've got away with it for another week!'

Robinson's desire for involvement in a project is indicated by his political activism and in his participation in Equity, the stage union. 'I think I have always been a bit of a Utopian,' he says. 'I always thought I didn't want to be one of those people who moaned about stuff and at the end of my life looked back and thought I moaned about it and never tried to change it.' It seems to him, he says, utterly obvious to try to change what is apparently wrong, and he has never understood other people who don't.

Boldness: sticking your head on the block

Successful people are daring. Some of them literally risk their lives to take on a challenge. Tony Bullimore, whose survival almost defies belief, almost lost his. Boldness, however, is always part of the make-up of the brilliant. Sebastian Coe, never in danger of his life but often in danger of failure and humiliation, hesitates only when asked to define what sets a champion apart from the rest.

> The one thing I'm always aware of is paperback books that have 10 pointers to being a champion. Everybody is different; we're all moti-vated by very different things, for extrinsic reasons and intrinsic reasons. Some people want to be successful because they like the idea of

having a big house and a Porsche on the drive; others want to do it to explore how hard and how mentally tough they are.

For most of us it's probably a mixture of all those things. If you ask me, the one continuum that runs through all those different models is just, actually, the bloody-minded self-determination to be better than the next person. To sometimes be able to prove a point and to just be able to explore, it's a voyage. It's actually being interested and excited and wanting to explore and perhaps pick up the stone and find out what's underneath it. To some people that's uncomfortable, being prepared to stick your head on the block and know you're going to be publicly examined if you set off in pursuit of something.

Rather than buckling under pressure, Coe thrives under it. 'The real thing that excited me was major championships,' he says. 'I always knew the difference between going into a year where there were big races but no major championships, and going into a year when I knew that in August I was going to defend an Olympic title or hope to win a European title.'

Coe was the outstanding 800-metres runner of his day, but failed to win an Olympic medal in that event (although he won two silvers). 'I would have loved to have won the Olympic title, but I'm not somebody who sits back and thinks what might have happened. It's probably one of my failings that I move on quite quickly. I never go back.'

Comfortingly for ordinary mortals, Coe says that half the struggle for success is through application. Less happily, the other half of the struggle to win in competitive sport is probably inbuilt.

Without getting boring and scientific about it, I do have a very low heart rate; I have a very large capacity for oxygen uptake... I have a light frame and I always ran in balance. That was the luck of the draw. I don't think that in itself it would have been enough to get me beyond being a useful national standard competitor. The difference between that and getting on to a rostrum for major championships is 80 miles a week, 10–12 hours in the gym and all the other things that go with it.

The single-mindedness in Coe's character emerged again when he resolved to go into politics. This came as a surprise to many, but Coe had been fascinated by politics since he was a teenager and had intended to make it his career until running took over. He joined the Conservative Party and was almost immediately selected as the parliamentary candidate for Falmouth and Camborne. He gained the seat, only to lose it again five years later in the New Labour rout.

Like Coe, Roger Black is single-minded; all top athletes, he says, have to be bold:

> Metaphorically, you need to have a big heart and big balls, to be honest. The 400 metres is an event that most people will not try because it hurts. If you can imagine training for something and doing something that you know will hurt you, that is why most athletes won't do it. Lactic acid is created more in the 400 metres than any other event, so sometimes the races are really great because the training is so hard. Psychologically, to do something five or six days a week, knowing you won't be able to walk at the end and that you're going to be sick, and that it will take two hours to recover, frightens quite a few people off. You have to have a warped sense of perspective and that's why somebody like Iwan Thomas, the British number one, is somebody you don't bet against. He has such a great head; he just wants to get in there, he has no fear.

Natural conquerors: defeat not an option

Is defeatism inbuilt? Conversely, are some born with a belief that nothing will stand in their way? This may be a quality that grows with achievement, but it begins as a disposition. Whatever made Chay Blyth believe he could row across the Atlantic when it had not been done this century? 'At the time, it seemed like a good idea,' he says. 'It was my first trip at sea. We had done a lot of specialization in the regiment in survival – desert survival, Arctic survival, that sort of thing, so sea survival seemed like quite a good idea.'

Having learnt to row, he could see no reason why he shouldn't be a good sailor too. As he told *Lloyds List*:

> To begin with, I knew nothing about sailing. I couldn't even navigate. I thought I'd teach myself as I went along – and I did – which got up the

noses of the bar-room gin-and-tonic brigade because it destroyed the cosy image that sailing is élitist and takes a lifetime to learn. To me, the ocean was one of the last great challenges. I thought rowing, sailing – can't be much different.

Switching off: the tidy mind

Intellectual energy is a hallmark of brilliant people. Chay Blyth says his strength has been 'recognizing an opportunity and being able to take advantage of it'. Then he adds: 'They present themselves almost on a daily basis – well, they don't present themselves, because I look for them.' But those who intend to combine a brilliant career with a life outside work also need to be able to switch off. Sebastian Coe was forced to do this by his siblings, who chimed 'boring, boring' when he and his father got on to athletics at the dinner table.

Nicola Horlick believes this skill is very important:

> One thing I have observed over the years is that people who do it successfully are able to think about work when they are at work, and home when they are at home. They are very good at switching on and off in that way. If you're in the office and you're constantly on the phone to the nanny because you don't trust the nanny, or staying up all night cooking the food because you don't trust the nanny to cook the food, or just generally interfering non-stop with what the nanny's doing, you shouldn't be doing it. You should actually be at home. Similarly, when you're at home, I think it's very bad if you're constantly working and telling your children to come back later when you've finished writing this note or whatever. It is incredibly important to choose the right career to make sure it can fit.

There are myriad other qualities that appear, in small or large part, in our brilliant careerists. We see extraordinary _sang froid_ in Tony Bullimore, who, having spent five days in a wrecked boat hundreds of miles from land, required only a couple of pints with ordinary humanity to recover from the trauma. 'There are times when I think I would need a good mate or family around me and that would be if someone extremely close to me got very ill or died. I'd be more weary and upset if that happened,' he says. 'In these situations, I just look at things very cold-bloodedly. You put yourself into this situation. You know the old saying – if you can't stand the heat, don't go into the kitchen.'

We see extraordinarily sunny natures – Robin Smith and Roger Black are examples – and the ability to be philosophical about criticism. We see a disinclination to complain, and to be positive (Roger Black, despite his illnesses and his congenital heart defect). We see theatricality (Tony Robinson, a natural performer); and, of course, we see tremendous egos!

Without the ambition to do well, any amount of natural talent will wither and waste (and Sebastian Coe talks in Chapter 3 about the youngsters he has seen with prodigious inborn talent but no will to use it). But of all our characters, the two who perhaps combine the most unusual blend of characteristics for hugely successful people are Robin Smith and Michael Lynagh. Both natural sportsmen – and, like many sportsmen, talented in more than one sport – they are also modest, self-effacing and apparently without ego. Lynagh attributes his achievement to fabulous luck (at 'having a lot of natural talent, and I mean that in the most humble way').

Lynagh also acknowledges that, on the field, he had the mental ability to assess the game all around him, spotting opportunities and chinks, even as he played in it. And although he is quiet, he is also ambitious, competitive and driven.

In a very quiet and unassuming way I am a very driven person. When I set my mind to doing something, it normally gets pretty well done. I can remember as a kid my father would say to me, 'Just take it easy.' We used to go on summer holidays down the coast and if I wasn't watching cricket on the TV I would be out surfing, then there would be tennis on another channel, which I'd watch. After that I'd say, 'I want to go out and play tennis and see what this tennis lark is all about.'

Until Dad actually took me to a tennis court and got me a racquet I would bug him. I actually believe I was a little bit over-competitive in my early days – a pain in the arse, actually, but it got me to where I was.

Robin Smith was less doubtful about his own talent, but is equally self-effacing. He has been happy to restrict his competitive urges to the game; he has never been tempted to move from Hampshire by offers of better contracts; he was surprised to be offered the captaincy; he has never been especially ambitious; he is rarely confrontational. Most of these characteristics would militate against a brilliant career without Smith's extraordinary natural talent. He broke 30 school athletic records, was South African under-17 shot put champion, a swimmer, a national standard rugby player. He may be modest, but as he says, 'I don't want to sound arrogant; talent is something you're blessed with.'

Great expectations – the influence of hearth and home

Had it not been for a little accident with a knitting frame – or, more precisely, two largish accidents with a knitting frame – Sir Chay Blyth could have been something big in Scottish knitwear. It was the second accident that finished his budding career with Lyle & Scott, a concern that flourishes without him.

Blyth left school, as did his peers, at the age of 15. The youngest of seven children in a working-class family, he was not from a background that fostered yachting adventures at sea:

> There were teddy boys and people like that [around at the time], and we were just a wild bunch. Where I was working, there was a frame about the width of a room, and as an apprentice it was accepted that at some stage of the game you'd bust the machine. But if we did something wrong it didn't just stop, it crunched up and there was a lot of damage. I bust the machine – but a week later, I bust the machine again. The foreman – who hadn't got a sense of humour – kept on poking me, and unfortunately poked one time too much.

After the contretemps with the foreman, Blyth joined the Parachute Regiment. It was a tough environment, which was to prove his making. He responded to discipline and challenge, and became a sergeant at the age of 21, the youngest-ever platoon leader in the regiment at the time. The Army came as a shock to Blyth – not least the expectation of such physical effort – but it was to bring out the qualities that propelled him to success. He was in the Army when he undertook his first challenge at sea: rowing the Atlantic with John Ridgeway, a captain in the same regiment.

> I've got nothing but good to say about the Paras. The training was just fantastic; they demanded and expected 100 per cent loyalty, and they got it. It taught us tremendous things in terms of discipline, tenacity and to know that, when it comes to really severe conditions, it's your mind that'll go first and not the body. As long as you keep the mind going the body will just follow along happily. It probably taught us focus as well. It was a huge culture shock for me, having come from the Borders, unable to string three English words together. I suddenly found myself in Aldershot, and I'd done no exercise at all. On one occasion I'd swum for the south of Scotland, but only once, and that's because the person went sick and I was the only reserve. I'd done no running, so when they used to talk about 12, 15 miles you used to think, 'Jesus!' But it helped tremendously with discipline.

Without the Army, Blyth may never have left the Borders, but the chances are that he would. The influence of hearth and home are significant, but, as our subjects indicate, parental ambition is likely to be effective only if the child is receptive. Inborn qualities and talents can be nursed and nourished, but strong-minded individuals will go their own way. Interestingly, however, while some of our subjects received enormous support and encouragement from home, and others received hardly any, none was actively discouraged from pursuing the career they had chosen, even if it resembled nothing like their parents' expectations.

Nicola Horlick's mother, a qualified architect who never practised after her marriage, encouraged her daughter to continue to work after having children. As is well known, Horlick went on to have six children and continued to work through the severe, and eventually terminal, illness of her eldest daughter, Georgie. We will explore her rather unconventional motives later, but she had been reassured by her mother's support.

It was partly the age that she lived in, partly that my father was very anti her working. He felt he should provide for her, in a very old-fashioned way. She felt it was not the right thing to have done, she has always felt that. She has always encouraged me; she felt terribly unfulfilled that she hadn't achieved anything in life. I think she achieved something in that she brought up two children very well. She has always encouraged me to go on working and admits that she was pretty bad tempered and difficult because she felt unfulfilled. I think I would probably be the same – I'd be quite difficult.

Harvey Goldsmith was building up his career as a promoter while his parents believed he was committed to becoming a pharmacist. Asked whether they objected to his change of direction, he responds: 'Well, I have no idea!' Evidently, the senior Goldsmiths were not invited to comment and even left in blissful ignorance as their son carved out an alternative path. Yet the signs were there: he had started a jazz society in the sixth form at school, and part of the reason he chose his college, Brighton College of Technology, was because he had been told it had a fantastic social life. It didn't. Then his degree course was stopped after six weeks, and he had to reregister to do an external London degree. It was supposed to be excellent, but the lustre had gone off it for Goldsmith.

It wasn't the course I wanted to do and I got disillusioned with it at a very early stage. Part of the reason I wanted to go to Sussex was that I was told it had this fantastic social life. I went to my first union meeting (I got nominated because I happened to be the last person in one Friday morning for a lecture) and listened what was going on – the cricket tour, the rugby tour – and then there was time for questions. I stood up and said, 'I'm from pharmacy.' They all laughed. They had never seen a pharmacy rep before at a union meeting. I said, 'I've been here six or seven weeks. I was told this was a great social place but nothing's happened.' There was murmuring and a slight rumbling...

At the end of a mildly acrimonious discussion, the union president issued the usual challenge: if he was such a social animal, why not open a club himself? Club 66 (it was 1966) opened in January in the refectory and common room. The lights were dimmed, a couple of acts were booked, and nuts and crisps were placed on the tables. It was an instant success, first on Friday nights, and then Thursday nights as well. Goldsmith became rag chairman, then social secretary. He ended up with a secretary and an office and was running the entertainment for about 10 colleges and universities along the south coast. He put on *The Family* and the *Moody Blues*, moving to bigger shows. The rag ball moved to the Metropole, lasted all night, and attracted 4,000 people, dining, dancing and having breakfast.

> At that point we met and put on the John Mayall's Blues Breakers. They were backing John Lee Hooker, a great American blues artist. In the band was a guitarist called Eric Clapton. I got friendly with Eric, and he ended up coming down to stay with me over the weekend. To the great fancy of the rag queen at the time, he brought down Stevie Winwood, who at that time played for Traffic. I gradually built up a relationship with a number of artists, and it started to take over my life.

Tony Bullimore was:

> a typical war baby. My family thought the most important thing in life was to be able to go out and get a living and earn money and make something of life. Our route was to get into business. It wasn't academic. My biggest ambition was to get out of school as quickly as possible and get on with building a business.

This he did – and it enabled him to do what he loves to do: sail boats.

Ken Bates made his fortune when he left his father in the family haulage business, moving to Lancashire and building up a chain of quarries and ready made concrete plants. But as a child, Bates was already a single-minded individual. He wanted to be a professional footballer (and, in fact, played for Arsenal juniors) and when he left school, decided to go into a job where he would have enough spare time to pursue that aim.

> In those days, local government wanted to recruit more intelligent people – fast track, good people running the country. I went in and was

stuck in the surveyors' department. But I noticed that however important you were in the surveyors' department, you stuck a little piece of
paper under your arm and went across to the treasury department. So I
said that was not for me, and got transferred.

Even there, however, local government was proving a disappointment for Bates. His boss heard him describe a wage of £7.50 a week as
chickenfeed. This would have been less of a mistake had his boss not
been earning precisely that, so as Bates stared towards his future with
the local authority, he could see only a cul-de-sac. He left and joined
British Rail, spending nine weeks there – seven of them looking for
another job. At 18, he plumped for accountancy, and met his first
influential person: a tough senior clerk. 'I joined an old City firm and
was given one of the toughest senior clerks to work with. He taught
me more in two years than the average articled clerk learns in five.'
He also, some would say, shaped the professional _modus operandi_
with which he feels most comfortable.

Sebastian Coe probably best illustrates how potent parental influence can be, provided it runs with the grain of an existing, or even
latent, ability. Coe's father, Peter, was his athletics coach, and Coe is
outspoken on the need for government funds to go into paying for
excellent coaching for fledging athletes. A cheapskate attitude to this,
he says, can never be counterbalanced by hyperbole. Athletics is so
demanding that the support of parents – although most of them
would lack Coe senior's single-minded dedication – is almost a
prerequisite for success. 'Any coach will tell you if they've got
parents on board, they're already halfway down the road,' Coe says.
'Any teacher will tell you that if you've got parents interested in their
child's development, progress is certainly helped rather than
hindered.'

Coe's father once said that he had put 'a hell of a lot more into
creating the athlete than I did creating the son.' Coe says this is partly
true:

I would not have been as good an athlete or competitor had I had a
different coach. He was 20 years ahead of his time. The testimony to his

coaching is the fact that the 800-metres record stood as long as it did. It stood from 1979 effectively, although I broke it again in 1981, until two years ago. No record has really stood that length of time, given the number of attempts there have been on it.

[My father] has the arrogance of an engineer who believes that most things have to be tested to destruction before they work. That's being a bit unfair because he also recognized, like a good manager, that you don't waste assets early on in the life cycle of a career. My training was geared very much to 10–12 years down the road all the time. He also was honest and sharp enough to recognize that as a good scientist, which effectively was what he was – he was also production director of two or three large companies – that you can't be skilled at every discipline.

In *Reflections on Success*, a series of interviews conducted by broadcaster Martyn Lewis, Coe said he could not separate his success from his background and upbringing. His father had been a competitor himself (a racing cyclist) and his mother, Angela, a repertory actress in Worcester and Birmingham. Coe's sister, Miranda, showed talent as a dancer and was sent to train with the Royal Ballet. Although Coe says they were 'a fairly ordinary family', there are clear signs that his parents went to extraordinary lengths to bring out their children's potential.

My father always had great aspirations for all of us and his view was always, I don't mind what you do; if you're going to empty dustbins just do it as well as you possibly can – be the best dustman around. There was never any pressure on us. One of the great things they brought to my career was more balance in my early years than I would have had otherwise. They were in a position to say what was important, as my father was coaching me and training me, but they were also never slow in saying, 'For God's sake get a life; go out and do something else for a bit.'

At the age of nine, Coe would run two miles into Stratford-upon-Avon to spend his pocket money, and back. His father began with engineering principles: 'He had learned from his engineering background that everything starts from fixed principles, and he was determined to apply the same discipline.' Peter Coe studied East Germany's athletics textbooks with dedication, then put them into practice on the windswept moors of the Peak District (the family had moved to South Yorkshire by then). Coe says: 'My father would finish work at six and for the next two hours we would be on the road or on the moors, me running in his headlights. During winter the weather was brutal, but it made me a better runner.'

Michael Lynagh's childhood was a tale of cricket and rugby league and his heroes were the greats of those sports. He was taken to his first rugby union Test match at the age of eight, but all he can remember are the teams (Australia versus the Springboks), the smell of protesters' stink bombs, and the police presence. His first sport was cricket, followed by rugby league, and his first experience of rugby union was when his family moved to Brisbane and his new school played rugby union in the winter.

> I didn't know the rules but I was happy to be out there on a Saturday morning with the rest of the guys doing something because I loved sport, I loved being involved. Cricket was the main thing and that was where I saw myself. Rugby started to become an interest when I was about 14 and I was playing in the under-14 B team at school. My school went from being a junior school to a senior school at 12–13, and we were joined by a lot of other kids. We had trials, and were divided up into four teams. I was fly-half in the B team. We had a particularly weak team, so I spent the whole day cover-defending tackles on the sideline near the corner post. The coach, in his wisdom, told me to cover number eight – I hated it, and that was why I got dropped to the Bs, because I hated playing number eight.

Meanwhile, Lynagh was playing in the first XI cricket team – but it was the first XV rugby squad that was going on a tour of New Zealand, and which he wanted to join. From the comparative mediocrity of the B team for his own age group, he trialled for the first XV and made the team.

> I made the team and I was fortunate enough to have a really good schoolboy coach and he helped me enormously. I played three years in the first XV at my school. In my last game for the school I broke my

collarbone. It was the third game before the end of the season and there was an Australian schoolboy's team coming to the UK, Ireland and America at the end of the year. I had my heart set on that and everybody was saying I would make it, no problem, because I had been in the Australian team the year before. I broke my collarbone six weeks before the trial. This was pretty devastating. You had to play in the trials to get on the tour. I managed to get better just before the trial, stood up in the trial and managed to get selected. That was my first summer out of school so there I was missing my cricket to be over here. When I came back from that at the end of January I got selected into the Queensland senior rugby team and that was it. The selectors did it for me and I haven't played cricket since, except for a couple of charity cricket matches here.

Lynagh was a contradictory blend: a quiet and unassuming child who was rabid about all sorts of sport, and competitive with it. His parents could see his natural talent but never forced him into anything. What they did do, however, was to encourage him to recognize that his ability was exceptional, whereas he tended to the view that he enjoyed his sport and himself but was 'nothing special'.

Every now and then I would get a pep talk from somebody. I remember when I was pretty young, about 16 or 17, and dad sat me down. He said, 'You've got something special.' I said, 'No, I haven't.' He said, 'Go and be confident, go and use it.' I remember little talks like that. My father and my mother were very supportive of my sporting endeavours when I was young. It didn't matter whether it was surfing, which I started when I was four, or anything else. I remember waking dad up in the morning and trying to persuade him take me to the surf or playing cricket or rugby or whatever I wanted to do. Whatever I wanted to do they were very supportive and they never really pushed me one way or another. They never actually pushed me into sport; they let me discover it myself. Discover it I did in a big way, I loved it!

Michael Parkinson, raised in Cudworth, near Barnsley, was also supported (and influenced) by his parents. At a tender age his father, a miner, who eventually died from silicosis at the age of 70, took him down the pit for the second time.

I had a great childhood – I was lucky with my parents. My dad was a miner, my mother was a housewife superstar and I was brought up in a very warm mining community. My father was a very remarkable man, a funny man, and had a great love of sport. He had left school at 12. He died at 70 from silicosis, which is something miners got in those days.

His father also took him to the local working men's club and introduced him to the broadsheet newspapers. Parkinson recalls the nurturing community formed by the pit bands, music and choirs. 'There was more popular culture around in those days than there is now in most middle-class families,' he says. But while his father was happy to inculcate a love of sport – which young Parkinson had, and still has – he was not expected to follow him down the mines.

Two things rescued me from the mines. One was my parents' determination that I wasn't going to do it, and the second was the 1944 Education Act, which meant kids like me, who could pass an examination, went to grammar school. I went to grammar school and it coincided with the nationalization of the coal industry. Of course, they came recruiting. I was taken down a pit by the National Coal Board and I came home and my father asked me where I'd been. I told him – down the pit, to Silkstone Colliery. 'What was it like?' he said, and I said, 'Well, you know, whitewash walls and strip lighting.'

The following Sunday, his father took him down his own pit, where he saw miners working nearly naked in a three feet six inch seam, in frightening heat.

He said to me when we got to the pit top, 'What do you think?' and I said 'No, no, never.' This was probably the defining moment of my life. He said, 'If I ever see you at the pit again, I'll kick your arse all the way home.' He was right. I had already decided - because I'd been to the movies and seen Humphrey Bogart – that I was going to marry Lauren Bacall, or Hedy Lamarr. I was going to live with Hedy Lamarr in a terrace house next to Barnsley Football Club.

Parkinson passed his 11-plus to go to Barnsley Grammar School, but it was despite the school that he went on to such success.

I was bad at school; not academic at all. I had two interests, one was writing and the other was playing cricket. I was part of that generation that didn't get a raw deal from education. We were allowed to go to grammar school for the first time, bright young working-class kids. The problem was it was wartime, or just after the war, and the young teachers had gone to war. In their place we were given these old reptiles from the Victorian age and they were bloody awful – they were brutal and they were sinister. I hated school. I hated school and couldn't wait to get away from it.

Raymond Blanc was also heavily influenced by his mother – a great cook – and his surroundings. He grew up in Besançon, eastern France, in a rural environment. 'As a result,' he says, 'my understanding of food is very deep and my style has always incorporated the wholesomeness of my mother's food.'

Imagine living in a completely unspoiled area with huge mountains and lots of rivers. I spent most of my childhood up to the age of 12 or 14 completely pure and unspoilt. The calendar would be subdivided into hundreds of different chases. I was a pure hunter/gatherer. The floor of the forest would offer countless offerings; ceps, morels, wild asparagus, girolle, berries of all kinds, snails, etc. The rivers and lakes would offer pike, trout and perch fishing, frogs, etc, all of which would be sold to the restaurant and provide a handsome income and a tremendous knowledge of the produce. My father also had a large garden and grew all the vegetables we ate at home. My mother would then apply her simple creative act of cooking. The table was the heart of the house.

England proved less of a nurturing influence for young chefs at that time. Blanc was shocked by the chasms between social classes, who had wildly different attitudes to food and eating – none of them very appealing. The social hierarchy meant that, as a waiter, he was at the bottom of the heap. 'My employer didn't look at me; I was a waiter and he looked through me. I was a non persona.' He was given a 'nasty little room' without proper sanitation, and a lousy wage. As an experience, he says, it was terrible.

England in 1972 was a very dark place, un-sensuous, concerning itself only with primary needs, especially where food was concerned. It seemed that the country had lost its drive, its pride. It was also a big shock as there were tremendously deep divisions between each of the classes.

Society did not give an opportunity for the working class to go up the social ladder so it remained in that safe place. Coming from a very working-class background, I could not understand this. Working-class people would never go in a proper restaurant, especially if it was foreign, even more so if it was French. They would prefer to go to the pubs and reinforce their working-class status by eating horrible greasy food to fill themselves up. Not only would they be ignorant about food but also prejudiced, and would condemn anyone going into a restaurant.

The bourgeoisie, as anywhere, was uninspiring, dull, nice and predictable – terribly boring. They went in restaurants not for the love of food but for socializing. It was improper to talk about the food you ate. The British protocol of table was so heavy that it…killed any form of joy.

The old bourgeoisie and aristocracy 'benefited' from the most refined and privileged education and, of course, they would embrace all the arts and certainly would love their food.

Yet, the produce was of poor quality. Despite being an island, the fish was four–five days old, there was no service, no quality of food and no freshness. Obviously, food was neither part of the British lifestyle nor of the culture.

At the Rose Revived, Blanc came in touch with a frying pan and food. This time he had befriended the chef who let him cook as an experiment. The boss, who had seen this happen and tasted Blanc's cooking, liked it so much that when the chef and his brigade went away, Blanc was offered his break. Six months after, he opened his first restaurant, Les Quat'Saisons, with his first wife Jenny. Blanc is totally self-taught and describes it as a 'great blessing'. 'I am not a blueprint of my own education; whilst missing the guidance of a masterful hand, I have gained in enjoying the freedom to pursue my curiosity; search and attain simplicity through complexity, freedom through restriction, harmony through conflicts.' It was not easy but he feels that he gained a lot. He is what he is because of that freedom. Too often, the master will craft you and shape you in his own image. If you look at the Blanc protégés, he points out, they are a diverse bunch. 'None of them is defined by the cuisine that I have taught them yet they still follow its principle. The reasons why are simple. My cuisine is eclectic, modern and open to experimentation but leans on solid traditional wisdom. This leaves the students free to choose.'

If Chay Blyth is at one end of the scale of parental influence, Tony Robinson is at the other. His father was a thwarted boogie pianist who had turned down an offer to play in a Forces dance band to stick with his steady career in local government in South Woodford. When young Tony showed a glimmer of theatrical talent, he suspects that his parents seized on it. Working-class East Enders, their own life had been conventional for its day: his father who passed examinations to enter London University was prevented from going because, as the younger son of a working-class family, there was no money to send him. His mother, meanwhile, kept house and 'knitted' while his father, who had become a junior administrator for London County Council, studied for examinations in the evening.

Tony was good at elocution. Every year, he used to take handfuls of prizes at the wonderfully named Wanstead Woodford Eisteddfod. When his parents saw an advertisement in the *Daily Express* for child actors for a musical in the West End, they submitted his name.

This is the only showbiz story I've got and it's really true … I had about six auditions and at the end of it, I was cast in this show. None of us knew that it would turn out to be something that would actually transform the whole of the West End – the musical was *Oliver*.

Prior to *Oliver* all the big musicals in the West End were American ones: *Carousel*, *Oklahoma*, *West Side Story*. No one thought the British could do musicals other than things like *Salad Days*, where everyone was terribly well-spoken. Suddenly, a new voice was being heard on the West End stage in music. It was in the same way that Harold Pinter, Wesker and Osborne had transformed what you might call the serious stage and suddenly I was part of this thing that was like a transforming agent and, for Britain, it was terribly important. There was all that stuff about the influence of America and the Marshall Plan and we couldn't get out from under their feet but suddenly we were able to do this stuff, so it was an enormous success.

After it had been on for about three or four weeks, the boy who was playing the Artful Dodger bunked off from school one afternoon and went and played football in the park, forgetting it was a matinée day. So they came to collect him and they couldn't find him anywhere.

Nobody thought of looking in the park. With a quarter of an hour to go they came up to me and said: 'Would you be prepared to go on as the Artful Dodger?' They hadn't yet had time to rehearse any understudies in the part.

You know what it's like when you're 12 or 13 – you have this extraordinary retentive memory. All of us could actually sing the whole show from beginning to the end – what pretentious little twots we were! We were all about this high and we all used to wear grey Robin Hood hats on one side and Marks & Spencer grey herring-bone car coats, with the collar curled up, and black shades. We used to smoke Peter Stuyvesant through white filters, at 12 and 13. So there was no problem about going on – I was cool! My dad worked at County Hall, which was just opposite the theatre, so I phoned him before the show was due to start and he dropped everything and came and saw me bluffing my way through the show. I can remember singing *Consider Yourself* drying stone dead, then humming the rest of the line.

Then they gave me the part of the understudy and after that, whenever the original lad was off, they let me play Dodger. That gave me an enormous amount of credibility as a child actor. I wasn't a star or anything but I was certainly marketable. For the next four years I had this extraordinary life; half the time I was at this co-ed grammar school on the fringes of London and half the time I was going into town and doing bit parts in movies with people like Judy Garland and doing bits of television. I was in *Stop The World I Want To Get Off* with Tony Newley. I was a really dysfunctional adolescent!

Robinson eventually left school at 16 with four O levels. His parents, especially his father, were still strongly in favour of him continuing to act. Instead of worrying about the insecurities of an actor's life, his father was deprecating of anything not connected with acting.

My father was a great boogie pianist. He played like Fats Waller. He spent most of the war up in Scotland as an NCO and playing a boogie piano with what was the Canadian Forces dance band. When the war was over they said to him, 'Would you like to come back to Canada and be a musician, or do you want to go back to South Woodford, where you've bought a semi-detached?' He chose the semi-detached South Woodford life.

I think when I showed a flicker of talent, he was excited for me; that in some way it allowed him to live vicariously the life he turned down. It was funny because in one way he wanted me to have the freedom to express myself, but in another way, he saw what my career should be. Anything I wanted to do that wasn't about acting he was very deprecating of. There was a great struggle between him and me. There was another me that I wanted to be but I always thought it was a bad me because my parents didn't like him. There was a me that he wanted me to be.

Robinson has steered away from following this course himself.

If ever I'm asked by young actors what I think they should do I always tell them to do lots of different stuff, because if you're only an actor, then what is the raw material you've got to work with? So many young actors are so obsessed with their career that actually, their lives are very thin, and I think that's very sad. I think one of the interesting things about that new influx of alternative comedians and performers like Ken Branagh and Emma Thompson, and a contributor to the enormous success they have had, is that they have actually lived lives – whereas my generation of actors tended to go to drama school at 17 or 18 and then become an actor and always remain an actor.

Although his background had been in musicals, he aspired to the comic-intellectual circles inhabited by performers such as John Fortune, John Wells, Eleanor Bron, the early David Frost, Willie Rushton, John Cleese and Michael Palin. 'They were glorious. I just wanted to be around them. I thought I could be happy for the rest of my life if I could be around that stuff and I felt I had something to contribute.' Having left school at 16 – whereas most of those people had been to Oxbridge – there was little chance of his breaching this charmed circle. Then *Blackadder* came along. No one, apparently, wanted the part.

They were desperate, they needed somebody for the pilot. Someone had seen me being small and vaguely amusing in a television show and said, 'Well, he could do it', and they got me in. It was wonderful. I can remember going on the train for the first series, a lot of which was filmed outside Alnwick Castle, and John Lloyd [the producer] said to me and Tim McAnelly, who played Percy, 'So what's it going to feel like to be famous?' We didn't understand that he was serious, and yet it was extraordinary.

I'm glad fame happened to me relatively late in life, I was in my mid-to-late-thirties by the time it happened and [I knew by then] that it was not Bosnia – it is not actually that important. I had had a partner who had had breast cancer. I'd had two children, I'd been through all these things that you do by the time you are in your late thirties, and deep down I know what's important. When I forget that, it's a bit sad and a bit pathetic. I think that if I'd had any fame and been a celebrity earlier on, and hadn't known what was important and hadn't known how to be rooted, I think I would have done an awful lot of drinking and been dead by now.

Once I was in *Blackadder*, everyone in television assumed that I had been to a rather good public school, then to Oxford or Cambridge, probably read classics, got a second because I was just too lazy and interested in other things to get a first and was a superb writer. So suddenly, by being this most idiotic cretin, I got this spurious cred. This really was how they viewed people like Stephen Fry, Hugh Laurie and Richard Curtis, and it wasn't me at all. I got it and I'm only too happy to hold on to it. I didn't go in and say, 'I'm sorry, I'm just ignorant.'

The finale in this chapter on hearth and home, however, must go to Robin Smith or, more precisely, to his father, John. Robin Smith was talented – no amount of encouragement will result in any schoolboy breaking 30 athletic records, playing rugby at junior Springbok level or becoming the under-17 shot put champion of South Africa. Smith senior, though, is the name that crops up again and again in this story. His level of commitment to the excellence of Robin and his elder brother, Chris – who also played cricket for Hampshire and England – was absolute.

Chris was the first to come to England to play cricket after a friend in South Africa, Barry Richards, who played for Hampshire for many years, encouraged him. Chris came in 1980 and played for one season. When Robin left school, Richards suggested a four-week trial. Smith senior paid for the ticket and said it would be a wonderful experience and even if it did not work out, it would be a holiday (it actually turned into a 19-year stay).

> My dad has been an enormous influence and the success I've achieved I would put down to his total dedication in developing me from an early age. My father was totally dedicated to his business and to developing my potential as a cricketer and sportsman. When I was 10 or 11 years old, we used to wake up at 4.30 every morning and whether it was athletics, cricket or rugby, we would go out and train every single morning. He tried to do it with my brother, but because my brother is a lot stronger, he just said, 'Bugger that, I'm not getting up!' I'm a different person. I just love and respect my dad and I did everything, even if I didn't enjoy it. All my other friends didn't have to get up, and during the school holidays they would go off partying, but my dad was totally dedicated to making sure I was a successful sportsman.

Smith adds: 'I absolutely adore my folks, and now that I have two children of my own, I can appreciate how special I might be to them, and the sort of love and work you put into your kids.' The five-year age gap between him and his brother precluded jealousy: 'My brother has always acknowledged that I had a lot more potential and talent than he had.'

At the age of 17, the talented (and well-coached) Smith was already rubbing shoulders with cricketing greats. His nickname, the Judge, comes from those days. At the age of 17, he was playing his first first-class game against Western Province in Cape Town. Alan Lamb – who later played for England – also played in the same game.

I was about 30 or 40 in, and in those days my hair was longer. The curls were tight and they looked liked a judge's wig. Lamb was getting quite frustrated that this 17-year-old whippersnapper was batting away out in the middle. Garth Lerue was coming in to bat and Lamb said, 'Oi, Garth, run and knock that bloody judge's wig off his head!' I went into the bar that evening and Lamb called over, 'Oi, Judge, would you like a drink?' From then on, it stuck.

3

The learning curve – the skills that characterize brilliant careers

The first thing in starting out in business is that you have to believe in what you're doing. The second is don't take no for an answer. The third is never look at the sky; look at the downside, because the blue skies are always there, but you must calculate your risks, because if the risk factors are right, the rewards will be there.

Harvey Goldsmith, concert promoter

We have looked at characteristics that predispose success, at the varying family backgrounds against which our brilliant careerists began, and at early influences that may have contributed.

There is, however, a third important factor: the skills that can be acquired by deliberate effort. Some of these are hard to place clearly on either side of the nature–nurture divide. Take doggedness. Are you born dogged, or do you acquire doggedness? Probably a bit of both. An energetic disposition may predispose someone to work hard, and a careful nature may foster thoroughness. Even passion can be developed, to an extent. Some people are struck by their passion as they amble through life – Raymond Blanc was as he stood entranced in a French square, watching a head waiter flambé fish at a table – but for others, passion develops through other avenues and slower beginnings. Some people more naturally take risks, but caution can be abandoned by decision.

The killer combination occurs when individuals set out to capitalize upon their natural propensities and talents, by polishing and honing the qualities they have detected in themselves (or others have detected in them). Under-exploited talent is not enough; great effort without innate talent will get you further. But brilliant careers come from a happy combination of both. Harvey Goldsmith, asked for three tips for anyone starting out in business, came to the same conclusion in his response above. The three broad stages of attaining a brilliant career are the vision, the persistence and the application.

It's not that easy, of course. Many different qualities go into each stage: imagination, seeing opportunity, audacity, persistence, hard work, determination, seizing chances. Promising starts have to be sustained by thoroughness, preparation and discipline. Sometimes these factors slip around in the order of things; some feature more strongly than others; but most are always present.

There is another thread running through our successful careers, and this is harder to define. It is running your own race; being aware of the competition in the field without being cowed by it. It is a realization that you cannot control what other people do, only what you do yourself. It is about having courage, if you like.

We have called this section the learning curve and have allocated it three headings: design, determination and diligence – the three interdependent facets of brilliant careers.

Design

There are plenty of athletes who you can see from relatively young ages have precocious talent but fall through the net. Sometimes this is because they just are not prepared mentally to commit to it. That's not a macho statement. If they're not prepared to do that, they'll be much happier going off to do something else. There's nothing worse than seeing people in sport at 14, 15 and 16 being pushed into something that really doesn't interest them and they don't want to commit to.

Sebastian Coe

No one ambles casually into a brilliant career. No one is casually brilliant, no matter how laid back they may appear. Every brilliant career involves a passionate desire to follow it. Without this, innate talent goes to waste. All of us have seen people who have great talent but not a lot of desire to use it – as Coe says, not everyone is sufficiently motivated to exploit even prodigious talent.

Our subjects, though, did. The first step towards a brilliant career is coming across that magical thing: the thing you really, really want to do. It is to know what you want. It can be discovered by logic or by gut feeling. It can be a natural talent or a straightforward desire (which is harder, and which perhaps requires more perseverance).

Our subjects illustrate that both ways will work. They are motivated. How does one acquire motivation? There's a harder question. Tony Robinson is probably not typical. He has said he had a desperate desire to prove his worth. Why? 'I think part of it is from being small,' Robinson says. 'I think being a small bloke you are confronted at school by all that games stuff and all that lad stuff.'

Being small – not a quality most people hope for in their sons or themselves – can therefore be a spur? Robinson says that the strategies one evolves to avoid being bullied, another age-old phenomenon, can be invaluable.

> I wasn't bullied very much; I learnt routes round it. You don't have to think that just because you are red-headed or short-sighted or spotty or short that necessarily you are going to be bullied. There are strategies, and I think those strategies are often very useful in later life. I think that's true for Rowan [Atkinson]. He was that gawky little kid with the big ears and when people decided to bully him he would make them laugh. Then when he'd survived to the sixth form they realized how interesting he was.

Looking at motivation, even from such a small sample as our subjects, shows that there is no such thing, in fact, as a typical motivational factor. Take Nicola Horlick, who says she possesses energy rather than drive. Her motivation for going out to work, and throwing herself into her work, was connected largely with the fact that her eldest daughter was diagnosed with leukaemia at the age of two. If that had not been the case, Horlick says, she would have spent her waking hours dwelling on the awful possibilities of what might happen. Finally, Georgina could not defeat the illness and died at 12. Work, Horlick says, took her mind off of it.

Sebastian Coe had never analysed his own motivation until the day he decided to retire. As he told Martyn Lewis in *Reflections on Success*: 'What drives successful people along is that perfection is always around the corner.'

> I wasn't sure what it was that actually really motivated me until that day. Then it became very clear. I used to live in Twickenham on the river and I used to run the towpath in the mornings. I remember this as if it were yesterday: I was running on a November morning and I suddenly came to the conclusion that I would never probably be able to run any quicker. At the start of every new season, roughly October or November, I was always able to sit back and think I could probably lift more weights or I could do something different in the gym. I could do a bit more speed work or perhaps a bit more mileage, or perhaps come off the mileage. There was always something I could picture myself doing differently. That day, for the first time in my career, I realized that there was nothing I hadn't tried now. Although I knew I could probably run pretty quickly for two or three years, the realization that I wouldn't run any more quickly, that I wouldn't improve on any of my times, gave me the clearest signs to the door.

Coe is not a short man – but size, once again, does matter! He had good natural balance, slow heart rate, a light frame and a large capacity for oxygen uptake, but he had been told he was too small to be an 800-metres runner.

> I was told when I was 18 that I was too small, not tall enough to be a good 800-metre runner. I rather enjoyed proving them wrong there. I was told that I was more a distance runner and would never make a 1500-metre runner and I rather enjoyed proving them wrong there too. I think those sorts of things are probably all part of it.

Roger Black (who is tall) never had anything to prove. He lacked what he calls the classic motivation. In fact, it took him a long time to understand his own motivation.

> My motivation to run was not the classic sports champion's motivation – so many are motivated basically to move away from pain, they had a bum childhood, with abuse and racism. I come from a comfortable background. It took me a lot longer to work out what it was about me. To come back from my injuries and illnesses was one thing. Mostly, I recognized the talent I was given, that there were people out there with as much talent but worse injuries. Most importantly, my desire was to reach my full potential. To look back and say, 'If only I had done that in my day' would have been so sad.

Black is now a motivational speaker and has studied the elements of this elusive phenomenon. He also faced a personal challenge after his own retirement: to find something else that would give him the same impetus and inspiration as athletics had. He told Simon Smith of _The Daily Telegraph_ in 1988:

> My career has stopped a few times already. The problem isn't what to do. The important thing is to do something I'm passionate about, which is what athletics has given me – that daily knowing what I'm about. I'm not foolish enough to try to replicate standing on the Olympic rostrum. What I have to try to replace is the process athletics gave me – the reason, the focus which athletics gives you every day.

Black takes his motivation from every and any source:

> I've read a lot of books about motivation. When I have conversations with people, I'm looking for something that can make a difference to my life. When I read certain books I don't think you have to get all of it, just one piece of information.

For those possessed by passion, the process is less scientific: they want it, they do it. Michael Lynagh was desperate to play sport (any sport, whether it was surfing or tennis). He badgered his father to take him (although he didn't always get his own way). He played sport he wasn't especially keen on. He had a 'real competitive urge'. Others had to tell him that his talent was outstanding; but it could be left to his own obsession with sport to ensure he carried on playing.

Raymond Blanc remains irradiated by passion. Throughout, his career has been a delicate balance between what he passionately wants to do and what he is obliged to do by commerce. To be a top chef, Blanc points out, requires nothing short of passion.

We are all a bit mad. All chefs are mad creatures. You need to be a bit mad because who wants to work 18 hours in a dark kitchen under tremendous pressure at great speed? Every guest is expecting great things every lunch, every dinner. Imagine giving 12 or 14 shows a week. You would be absolutely exhausted, and we are exhausted. It is a tremendous physical demand and also stressful to combine commercial responsibility, creativity and leadership.

All that I do at Le Manoir aux Quat'Saisons is lead by ideal, but at all times it must translate into commercial gain. The commercial side does not come first. Ten years ago I went to Japan for the first time. It touched me completely; everything about Japan but mostly the expression of their art. The beautiful food, pottery, painting, etching and of course their wonderful gardens. Visiting one of the gardens in Kyoto, I decided to create my own at Le Manoir. The cost was high (£200,000) and the work required 200 tonnes of stones to establish it plus the skill of an expert in Japanese gardens. So I decided to create a Japanese festival of art. We created a magnificent Japanese garden (*Fugetsu-An*) and we invited some of the greatest artists, sculptors, painters, chefs, musicians and singers from Japan. Every night for a week we had traditional Japanese opera. The Japanese ambassador and his wife came to open the festival. It was a great success but very costly and many people queried the wisdom of this investment. By creating that Japanese festival of art I was one of the very first to honour the Japanese culture. Subsequently, we were held in very high esteem by our Japanese friends and received tremendous press coverage (and still do today). By doing so we increased our Japanese guests by 4%. Although this was led by an ideal it provided its own return, plus all the fun and new knowledge.

Here we work and we aim as a team to touch the sublime. I would like to think of myself as a craftsman, not a businessman, and I have always relied on the skills and talent of managers and businessmen who understand my vision and will help me to realise it, and I think I have done very well. My partner, Richard Branson, is a rather well-known and respected entrepreneur, whose philosophy and success is also firmly based and rooted in people. That is the foundation of his achievements.

My success is also a reflection of the quality and professional support provided by my team and management. People who are the very best in their field, people who share a passion and have ownership in creating something truly beautiful. I am not trying to be the man of all trades or I would only become just that. At Le Manoir, my main activities are my craft and teaching; I am very much involved in the gardens and the interior design of the house. For both, create a refined and warm environment that is conducive to joy.

I try to look at things with new eyes each day; routine is a great killer. It grows cobwebs in your eyes and in your brain. Even if I have done a dish a hundred times, I will always look at it with interest and feel the challenge to make it better. I try to reinvent myself every day; as a young man I used to jump out of bed; now I have to do this more cautiously: but when I am up I feel the day is new. To be a champion for more than 25 years is tough and also unnatural. You have to fight constantly the force of entropy, which pulls you down all the time. You have to create a tremendous amount of changes in your approach to everything; technology, systems, people, trends, etc. As for management skills, I had to grow them as I did not have any. To understand my craft I learnt chemistry, which allowed me to understand all the denaturation process of my food, which I hope makes a far better teacher.

Even after 25 years, Blanc is still passionate about his cooking, his restaurant and about keeping the ethic of excellence. Le Manoir has just finished a huge programme of refurbishment, which now classes the hotel on par with the restaurant: one of the very best in Europe. It is this that has stopped him opening any sort of chain. He has, however, opened a small group of Le Petit Blancs – Oxford, Cheltenham, Birmingham and the latest in Manchester (autumn 2000). Asked why he did not expand earlier, he replied:

Because my life has always been led by ideal and not by commerce. If you had asked me 15 years ago, I would not have done it and I was probably right as I was not ready. I could only give myself to one place. How many castles can you have? How many Rolls Royces can you drive at the same time? How many mistresses can you pleasure? To me, at the time, it felt like greediness, like somebody putting too much food in their face. I am very proud to resist so long any form of expansion because it allowed me to give to Le Manoir so much of me; that is also the reason why it is such as success. To grow without sacrificing your ideals needs the best management and it is only now that we have the team and experience to do it.

Le Petit Blanc is to bring to the provinces what is much needed in the provinces. I don't want to create a chain because a chain has no soul, no heart. Le Petit Blanc is not a *petit* Manoir. It is a modern brasserie that welcomes families, the time-conscious businessman and the student alike. The food is of high quality (mostly free-range, and three of the brasseries have the Bib Gourmand Michelin) served in an elegant and modern environment. The service is warm and professional and very affordable.

Le Manoir aux Quat'Saisons is one of the best-known eating places in the country, but Blanc denies that it is élitist.

Elitism is often a reflection of the high price tag. In that way Le Manoir is a contradiction; it stands as one of the most expensive places in Great Britain, one of the very best but incredibly enough one of the most popular venues. We welcome 52,000 guests a year, and who comes? Yes, we have the rich and the famous, which is wonderful, but 50% of our guests come once a year or once in a lifetime to celebrate a special moment in their lives. We have succeeded in doing so by creating a culture of welcome and warmth, elegance but not luxury. At Le Manoir, you can open your jacket and also take it off as well. Actually, I have spent my life removing gentlemen's jackets at the table.

To me, the table is a very simple medium, a simple place, one of the very last places we can meet, tête-à-tête with our friends, our loved ones, and talk, relate to one another, get to know one another, give one another a bit of love, a bit of warmth. At Le Manoir I translate that great learning that is part of the simple philosophy of my parents. It is a place to celebrate life, even if it's slightly unrealistic, who cares?

Some years ago it was amoral to enjoy good food. There was a strong guilt tag to enjoyment. I met a wonderful priest who loves his food and he came to the restaurant twice. He used to come by himself and I said, 'Don't you find it a little bit dubious to come twice to the restaurant and enjoy yourself, for yourself?' He said, 'No, I can give more pleasure and more joy to other people because your meal makes me so happy. You put so much beauty into it at every stage, the professional part and the enjoyment part, so I can be a better man.' Put that way I could only agree with him.

Tony Bullimore's feeling for sailing is a passion, and it is intensified by his awareness of his age (he is in his 60s). 'Lord King gave up his chairmanship of British Airways at 70, 72, something like that,' says Bullimore. 'He actually went on to become chairman of another company after that. There are lots of people like that.' Bullimore was, at the time, building a 100-ft catamaran in Bristol, to challenge the 71-day, 13-hour Jules Verne round-the-world sailing record. Although he has spoken about retiring with his wife to Jamaica, he is not planning that yet.

Chay Blyth is passionate about sailing. Anyone who defies conventional wisdom from experts on a life-threatening pursuit has to be. When he attempted his first round-the-world sailing the wrong way, celebrated sailors wrote to him. With encouragement? No, with one exhortation: 'don't do it'.

A very famous French ocean sailor wrote to me and said don't go, it's impossible. We had no idea how long it was going to take. We had stores on board for 18 months. Nobody had any idea. In those days, during very bad weather, you used to turn and run in front of the waves and go with the wind. But we went, and we achieved it. The reason it took so long was because of Cape Horn. The boat was picked up on its side and smashed down and my self-steering gear was broken beyond repair.

What drove him to take risks and accept new challenges?

I'm not rabbiting on about the working-class element of it; the fact is you bounce from the working class to a project to another project. My contemporaries go back and look at me, having got a knighthood, and think 'Jesus'. My mate, who's an architect, looks at me and says, 'How the hell could you get a knighthood? You're pathetic!' It's a question of striving forward all the time, but again, it comes back to this other thing of seeing an opportunity and taking advantage of it. I can think of more projects now than we have time to deal with. I could churn projects out like sweeties.

Blyth prepares his ventures with care and gets through the inevitable challenges, including the crushing loneliness of being alone for long periods, by remembering his purpose.

The loneliness doesn't really come into it, because you're focused on the end product, and in the case of the British Steel, it was to sail around the world. It doesn't always happen. I'm not sitting here saying we've succeeded in everything. We've had a few failures, I'm afraid. But generally speaking, these things don't come into it, because you're looking at the end product all the time.

Willingness to go against the grain, and to stick to your guns when those guns are under attack, features strongly in launching a brilliant career. When Ken Bates realized that football had to change by generating income outside the game, and upgrading stadiums, he was at least 20 years before his time. In 1966, when he was chairman of Oldham Athletic, he wrote in the *Football League Review* of the need to provide proper facilities in grounds and to generate non-football income.

Later – but again well in advance of others – he had a clear vision of what would become Chelsea Village. When he bought the club in 1982, he walked around the ground with the secretary and commented on the potential of the west stand. At the time the ground beneath it was just mud, the legacy of the Mears brothers, contractors for shifting the earth displaced when the Victoria Line was built. Stamford Bridge was an old quarry; the brothers filled it up and kept building, ending with the stadium. Now, having exploited the site as well as the stadium, Chelsea is a leisure and property group, with hotels, apartments and conference facilities.

Roger Black says that it is vital to identify your goals, and then to write them down: 'All champions set goals. They don't just think about them, they write them down.' He is still setting goals:

My goals are quite simple: to be the best sports presenter I can be. I want to be better at my business and grow it. My third goal is to help sports people with psychological preparation. I absolutely believe that in one conversation, with certain techniques, you can change the performance of a sports person, because it happened to me in one conversation.'

If setting goals is relatively simple, staying focused on those aims is harder. So it is important to set realistic goals, especially in activities where only one person can be the best. Black says – and he knows – that pitting yourself against others, then berating yourself for not being the absolute best, is the wrong approach. At the Atlanta Olympics in 1996, having missed two earlier events, one through illness, he came second – a brilliant achievement, and not second best.

I remember going into those Olympics. I had learnt so much over the 12–13 years of my career that I was about as good as I was every going to be. When I stood behind the line I was absolutely ready to become an Olympic champion, but Michael Johnson was in the race. When I crossed the line I came second, and it was about an hour later that they put an Olympic medal round my neck. If I were to show it to you now, you would see a silver medal, but that night, for me, it was an Olympic gold medal. The most important lesson I had learnt was when I stood on the rostrum with Michael Johnson, the only difference between us was in height. We both felt the same. I learnt you don't have to have a gold medal to feel like an Olympic champion. When I went into the race I wasn't thinking about anything apart from running as fast as I possibly could. That's all it was about. In that race there were athletes as talented as me, if not more talented, and on paper I should have come fourth or fifth.

Black knows that if he had chased Johnson, he would not have won a medal.

> I saw other people do it and I realized that the only way I could defeat Michael Johnson was if he messed up. It is not a defeatist attitude, it is definitely the right attitude to have. People think I said I was running for second place. I never said that. Before the race, I never thought where I would come, I just thought that if I execute my perfect race, where I come will not be in my hands. I could have come first, I could have come seventh. I could not control how the others performed.
>
> All champions in the world of sport are pro-active. They don't waste time worrying or focusing on anything they cannot directly control. The most obvious factor is your opponent. The reality is that you cannot directly affect how your opponents run. There is no point in focusing on them. The classic example would be if you were running against Michael Johnson and half way round the track he suddenly puts in a kick. You have a choice: you either react and run with him and come last, or you don't focus on him and you do your own race. That ability to focus on the things you can control and influence, and not worry about those you cannot, is important.

Like Black, Sebastian Coe learned to apply his energy to his goals. He told Fiona Millar in the *House Magazine*:

> In sporting terms, I am a competitive personality, but I tend to switch off in other areas. I think that if you are very committed in one area, it makes you very equable in others. All energy is total, and to get uptight about things that don't really matter is a waste of energy. Most people at the highest level in sport are quite relaxed away from it.

Coe says that the most important race in his career was the 800 metres in Prague, when he came third.

> This is another great fallacy in sport, and other walks of life, that people think it is only when you win that you succeed. They think failure is automatically linked with losing – it isn't. I learnt more in finishing third in that one race than I learnt in the 10 or 12 years leading up to it. In the 800 metres in Prague I was running against Steve Ovett for the

first time in my career. I decided the only way I could beat him was to try to run the legs off him from the front because I wasn't quick enough at that time in my career to out-kick him. I ran the first lap faster than anyone had ever been through in an 800 metres. I went through in 49 and a bit and I got to 600 metres feeling quite good; then I got to 610 metres and I thought the world was caving in. I remember Steve came past me in the finishing strait and to his complete shock an East German came past both of us.

I then realized two things: first of all you never ever go into a race thinking about one other competitor, you recognize that there is a race and there are other people capable of doing things. You have to think about the whole field, you have to think about the whole of the market-place. Secondly, most people said I was absolutely mad to have gone through the first lap in what I did, but I probably would not have got a medal had I not gone through at that pace. The one thing I knew was I had one year, two at the very most, to get myself in training not only to go through the first lap slightly quicker but also to hold on for a second lap. That is exactly what I did in the winter of 1979.

I completely changed my approach to the distance work I was doing and the kind of speed and endurance work I was doing on the track. I broke the world record nine months later. If you ask me what was the foundation stone of my career, it was that race. For most people it would have been third place and it really wouldn't have mattered in the scheme of things.

Some jobs present a particular challenge to stay focused on goals: acting must be one of the worst. Tony Robinson had some good advice early on.

I may not have got any exams, but I got A-level hippy in the 1960s. In the 1960s I had an American traveller friend who said, 'Always plan, but never plan on your plans.' I think that is just top advice. I try to find a route through stuff, but things change. I always try to be really attentive to those changes and go with them. I think the problem is if you say to yourself, 'Next year I want to do a leading part in the West End. I want to be able to spend at least a couple of months in Los Angeles and see if I can get at least something in Hollywood.' If you do that and don't achieve it, but achieve a whole lot of wonderful other things, you are going to be frustrated and angry with yourself. Whereas if you think to yourself, 'Let's put that down for the game plan and then if something else comes up and it's glorious, I'll really surf with that and enjoy that', it may be 10 times better.

Robinson's greatest achievements, he says, have not been in acting but in writing his own material in unplanned career gaps.

Up until the time of the *Adder* I was unemployed quite a bit of the time and would sit watching television and talking to my children about television an awful lot. I began to have a very clear idea about what I thought could be on in that magic slot between 4.45 pm and 5.45 pm that children would really engage in. I found children's television comedy, which at the time came in the form of *Rentaghost*, to be one of the most hideous experiences any child could possibly undergo – these sad old producers who thought the epitome of comedy was post-war ENSA. So I had this idea to have a series about Robin Hood and his Merry Men, except the reality was that Maid Marian ran the gang, and Robin was a twit, and everybody was too embarrassed to say.

Part of the reason it got on television, of course, was because once the *Adder* happened, the office door was open to me. Until then, I had had that frustration, whatever ideas I had had, the office door was firmly shut. Marian was the thing I really wanted to do and it was my show. I could decide what was in it, I could cast it, I could decide what the special effects were, what the locations were, what behind-camera staff we would have. I did it all in collaboration with a great friend of mine, who was the director, but essentially it was my show. To see it on the television and to see it win all those awards, that was really something.

Determination

If you believe in what you're doing, there's always an angle some-where, and you'll find a route through it if you're dedicated. Never take 'no' for an answer, particularly with banks. There's a banker or an investor somewhere, even if the terms are difficult.

Harvey Goldsmith, promoter

In these days of the National Lottery, e-commerce millionaires and instant gratification, there is a danger in believing that brilliant careers are almost events of simultaneous combustion. Hey presto! Best in the field! Just like that! The reality is more prosaic. You may have luck along the way, but persistence is a better bet. The more competitive and desirable the field you wish to go into, the more determined you need to be, and the harder you need to try.

Some careers are founded on this quality – the determination never to give up – but all need it. More complicated is another necessity: the ability to conquer self-doubt so that it does not bring down a project or a plan that once seemed absolutely right. So audacity is another requirement.

Ken Bates, an inscrutable operator, battled with Marlow Estates for the ownership of the Chelsea ground, and almost lost it. Marlow Estates, however, were not allowed to know this and, he says, backed down first: 'We came quite close on two occasions, but they never knew that, and they went before I did.' Bates will not say whether his reputed stubbornness is anything to do with success: 'That's for others to say, but the only way you'll achieve success is to stick at it.'

Tony Bullimore is a perfect example of determination reinforced by audacity. As he says, he is so determined that he has to be persuaded away from a project by others. His motto – nothing is impossible and nothing is impregnable – is accompanied by self-belief. Asked whether he minds his image as something of a 'Del Boy', adept at ducking and diving, he replies:

> Why should I mind it? I could have gone in lots of directions. I've got an intelligent mind, a good broad spectrum of what business is all about, where I could have gone or not gone. People say I'm a bit of a wheeler-dealer but I do know quite a lot of very good businessmen who have made it. A lot of them are 'Del Boys' but they've all gone through the hard times, been persistent and got there in the end.

Bullimore's extraordinary self-possession (and it is hard to say whether this is innate or acquired) emerged after his rescue from the ocean. He had come within a whisker of death. His recovery technique was not to go in for protracted counselling but to enjoy the company of his friends and a couple of drinks in the pub. It may be a corollary of this extraordinary self-possession that Bullimore sees no reason why age should hinder ambition and enthusiasm.

> Age to me is a measurement like time is a measurement. People are as good as they are. Some people break down with age. They get to 60 – I'm 60 – and they say, 'I can't do that, I'm not as young as I used to be.' I find this incredible. You can hang on in there. I don't believe that burning your brain up, working on your body and getting on with it kills people – I think it helps to keep some types of people alive. If I dried up and just sat there, in a few years' time it wouldn't be good news.

Michael Parkinson has had some lucky breaks, as he says in other chapters. The confidence to believe in himself, however, came from the Army, in which he did National Service. He became the youngest captain in his regiment at the age of 21, rubbing shoulders with Sandhurst officers and the best of the public school system. The realization that he was as capable as they – or more so – gave him a confidence that has remained with him, and an attitude about social classes.

> They didn't know what to make of me, nor I of them, but it didn't matter. I learnt that, actually, I was as smart as they were. Fear is the greatest thing of all. It holds people back. Fear that you might not be good enough for the job; fear that somebody out there is better than you are, and it holds people back falsely. In this country it's a real thing because there is still a class system at work. There is privilege, and there is an underfelt of people who are talented and ambitious but who feel that they are second rate, or are made to feel second rate because of that privileged institution above them. They shouldn't, because it's there for grabs, and that's what [National Service] gave me. I looked at these guys and I thought the majority of them were pillocks, frankly, who didn't measure up. The ones that did were great, but there were an awful lot who were there under false pretences.

Billy Connolly once said that he had spent years trying to develop an interesting personality so that when he went to John Le Carré's flat for a party he would be able to fit in – and that was when he had been regarded for years as one of the most entertaining individuals around! Self-doubt can never be banished; but it has to be vanquished when it arises. 'Maybe once you're successful what you get is an ease, you are happier with yourself and feel pretty impregnable most of the time,' Tony Robinson says. 'But once that impregnability is undercut, you die.'

> I can remember I was doing a political speech once, and when I ride that emotion there's just no stopping me. I had ridden that emotion for about four or five minutes about some particular thing and when I finished the guy next to me murmured, very quietly, 'God, you are boring.' It was brilliant; it destroyed me utterly for the whole of the rest of the evening. It was like somebody had punched me in the stomach – but if someone doesn't know that route to demolish me, I do feel fairly impregnable as a bloke in public situations.

Michael Lynagh's determination to play sport was exceptional. Outstanding talent carried him onwards and upwards. But when he broke his collarbone as a schoolboy player, his quiet determination came to the fore. Broken bones would not obstruct him.

> In my last game for the school I broke my collarbone. It was the third game before the end of the season and there was an Australian schoolboys team coming to the UK, Ireland and America at the end of the year. I had my heart set on that and everybody was saying I would make it no problem because I had been in the Australian team the year before. I broke my collarbone six weeks before the trial. This was pretty devastating because you had to play in the trials to get on the tour. I managed to get better just before the trial, stood up in the trial and managed to get selected.

Chay Blyth was so set on his goal, to sail round the world, that he persuaded a friend to secure a boat for him, even though he only knew how to row. He could not sail, navigate or find a sponsor – but he did get the boat. A friend of his, Brian Cooke, persuaded Westfield Engineering in Poole to lend him one of theirs. He broached 11 times in a day and believed (then) that it was normal! But he did not give up.

It is this quality of staggering back upright after being knocked over, both literally and figuratively, that brilliant people share. Harvey Goldsmith knows this more than most, not only through the failure of his business, and his subsequent determined comeback, but in more than two decades of doing things differently.

Goldsmith believed from the beginning that success is for the single-minded. The single-minded will go to all lengths to get where they want to go, as he was demonstrating as a student. He was in the United States on a student exchange when he got fed up after a month, took a Greyhound bus to San Francisco and got off.

As we crossed over the Golden Gate Bridge, there was a park underneath with a mass of people, and something very strange going on, and music playing. I thought, 'This looks interesting.' I got out of the bus station and worked my way down to this park. There was a group called the Grateful Dead playing, a love-in with all these hippies, beads and flowers.

Somehow or other I managed to worm backstage and met the Grateful Dead. I'm a believer that if you want to do something and you believe it's right, you do it. They thought I was a bit strange. I don't think they'd met many English people. They took to me and I hung out with them for a few days. They were very naughty and would spike your drinks with acid. They were well known for doing it. You could have a glass or wine or Coca-Cola but you were never sure what you were drinking.

It was a very exciting city, and at that time a font of the hippy movement. I saw around the town fantastic posters advertising these shows at the Fillmore Auditorium and the Avalon Ballroom. I was fascinated by the art on these posters, the fact that they stood out from everything else on the street. It was the whole psychedelic art scene. I thought, 'I'm going to have a go at this.' I met Bill Graham [of Fillmore] and Chet Helms [of Family Dog and Avalon] and somehow talked about how I was the biggest poster distributor in Europe.

I came back with a contract to represent the Family Dog and Fillmore Posters, which I wasn't quite sure what I would do with. I then had a complete set of samples, which I would have liked to put on my walls. I had to do my final year at university, which I was feeling terribly uncomfortable about as I was behind with my course, spending too much time on the social scene. I decided once and for all in my mind that pharmacy wasn't really what I wanted to do.

As he was coming to this conclusion, he saw an advert in the _Evening Standard_ seeking a partner for a poster company in Kensington market. It was the time of Biba, Carnaby Street – the most creative period since the war. He met the poster vendor, they got on well and set up together. They commissioned artists to do a poster for the gatefolds in the middle of various magazines, such as _Oz_ and _International Times_, another underground magazine, in exchange for which they underwrote the magazines.

They eventually opened inside Kensington market, printing on the first floor, with a newspaper shop and a magazines and poster shop in the middle. Goldsmith was running around Europe collecting magazines and hanging out at a club in Margaret Street called Speakeasy. 'I got more sucked into the music business. My parents thought I was having a couple of months off from going to pharmacy school, but it just dragged me in.'

Goldsmith's first benefit concert, the 14-hour Technicolour Dream at Alexandra Palace, was to raise money for _IT_ magazine. It relaunched him into the music business, but he had only £50 from his college grant.

> We needed capital. We went to all the banks, but rock'n'roll wasn't for them at all, they just didn't get it. With my partner at the time, I lobbied Camden Council to have a youth-orientated opportunity for young people as part of the Camden Arts Festival. They gave us the Roundhouse and we started to promote shows there. Then the GLC came to us and offered us Parliament Hill Fields, saying 'why not have a concert there?' We presented three free concerts at Parliament Hill Fields with audiences of up to 75,000, with a total budget of £250. There are ways of doing it, although it's completely hairy. Slowly but surely we started to develop a business, still doing one-off events.

Crystal Palace came next, and events called garden parties. They booked Pink Floyd, the Faces and Mountain. They were in business, and they needed money. The banks did not want to know. The break-through came in the shape of father and son John and Tony Smith, who put up £100 for the licence, and the show sold out in a day.

> It was just luck – finding money to start a business today is as difficult as ever it was. If you believe in what you're doing, there's always an angle somewhere, and you'll find a route through it if you're dedicated. Never take 'no' for an answer, particularly with banks. There's a banker or an investor somewhere, even if the terms are difficult. If you budget correctly – and always budget on how much you can lose if it goes wrong – you'll be able to convince somebody to get involved with you. The problem then is when you reach success, everyone around you who puts money in becomes greedy, and you've got another fight on your hands.

Goldsmith changed the shape of the rock concert – ruling out 'the juggling act and the dog act'. With Deep Purple, he changed to doing two-hour shows, but it took him six months to persuade Rank to let him book the Hammersmith Odeon. Grateful Dead did concerts lasting for six or seven hours. When Goldsmith organized Live Aid with Bob Geldof, it was the first time that 16 hours of TV had been assembled at one go. Live Aid became one of the turning points of the late-20th century: the shaming of governments by performers. Pulling it off, however, required more than social mores.

> I got quite friendly with Bob Geldof. Punk was a horrible, disgusting era – a rebellion of ugly people, as I put it. There were two or three bands around then that were really quite extraordinary – The Jam, The Clash and the Boomtown Rats. Michael Buerk made a documentary for TV and it riveted everyone who saw it. Bob Geldof saw it, got together with Midge Ure [of Ultravox] and created a song, which they recorded and put out. It was a huge hit and the whole machinery started. In our part of the world people were living on the fat of the land and not knowing how to spend their money next; down the road, millions of people were starving and it seemed ludicrous. It wasn't just our

industry, a huge number of people were wondering what to do. There wasn't a mechanism for it.

Bob Geldof phoned me up one day and said, 'We could get some really good acts together and do a concert.' I was a bit busy, about to take George Michael and Wham! to China, and before that I was in America. I said I'd call him when we got back. Bob got more determined and started to drum up interest. The day after I arrived back from China, Bob phoned me to say he was coming to see me that afternoon. He didn't ask if I was available, he just showed up. He sat in the office and said we had to do a show at Wembley Stadium with Elton John, Phil Collins, Stevie Wonder, The Rolling Stones ... I thought he was nuts but he said he was going to do it and wanted me to help him.

He convinced me to do it. It was literally 10-and-a-half weeks from the date. I called Wembley and booked that date – I wasn't sure why it had to be that date, but it did – then we talked about artists. We didn't have any, by the way. Bob said we had to put it on television and do a telethon, the whole bit. I didn't know much about telethons except that they could be difficult and were usually organized from one year to the next in a set pattern. Bob persuaded me to call my contacts at the BBC and he marched in there, with no discussions, announcing that he was going to do two shows, one in London and one in New York, with 16 hours of TV.

At that point an hour on TV was the maximum you could get. Roger Laughton, the head of daytime programming, who had agreed to meet us, said he would try to get two hours and maybe revisit it for an hour in the evening. Bob literally smashed his fist on the table and said, 'You don't get it either – either it's 17 hours or we're off!' He just stormed out of the room. Roger looked at me and said, 'What does he mean by "off"?' I said, 'I haven't the faintest idea; I'm not sure where else we're going.' About two seconds later Bob poked his head round the door and said, 'By the way, I need an answer by Tuesday.'

To Roger's eternal credit, he actually got hold of whoever he had to talk to at the BBC and talked them into this idea. It was the first time that 16 hours of TV had ever been assembled in one go and we didn't have a single act apart from the Boomtown Rats. I can't tell you it was a nightmare, because it just happened. There wasn't time to think about it. We held a press conference at Wembley Stadium announcing 16 acts, of which only four had been confirmed. The thing took on a kind of rollerball effect that's hard to describe.

The career of a promoter is not easy. As Goldsmith says, it is a subtle balance between the artist, the public and the venue, and each must be considered. 'You have to be sure the public is getting a good show, the quality of entertainment, and the right venue.' To get that far, however, you need 'grit and determination. You have to rise to the challenge and never take 'no' for an answer.'

Diligence, discipline, hard work

I always have a great belief that if you keep your head down and work hard then somebody will recognize it. I have always been very anti-politicking generally because I just don't believe that gets you anywhere. It might get you somewhere in the very short term, but ulti-mately people who are very political do not succeed, and it is much better to show you are good at what you do.

Nicola Horlick

Keep your head down, work hard, be thorough, prepare properly, apply yourself to the task – old-fashioned words that, as it happens, are absolutely true. There is no substitute for hard graft. There is no short cut to thorough preparation. As Nicola Horlick says – and others corroborate later – you can wing it for a bit. But only for a bit.

Even experienced top-flight athletes can fool some of the people some of the time when they haven't put in the training they should have, provided they have the mental attitude that has made them good in competition (for, as Roger Black says, all champions love pressure). But not for long.

'Nothing in sport, nothing in life that is good and successful, is produced overnight,' says Sebastian Coe. 'It's a long, long road. I first competed in 1969–70, and 10 years later I was at the Olympic Games. Those were 10 years of hard, hard slog. Anybody who loves what they do tends to think of it not as a sacrifice but as a way of life.'

Michael Parkinson may make it look easy to prod and probe his celebrity guests, but this doesn't mean he treats his job casually.

Thorough research is the bedrock of his job, and a jobbing worker is how he regards himself.

> I get a wad of stuff and I read through it and read through it. I know more about people when I talk to them than they do themselves, but that's the trick. I only ever use, generally speaking, 20 per cent. But it's important to have the other 80 per cent. I always make the comparison that interviewing is a bit like being a driver in a car. If I sit next to somebody and I think he doesn't know who I am, he's asking silly questions, he thinks I'm somebody else, it's like being in a car with a bad driver. You think, 'Christ, they're going to crash any minute.' If you're with a good driver, you are reassured immediately.

Parkinson has been successful himself; so have his guests. He has a perspective on brilliant careers from two angles.

> I think there are two things that make people successful. One is not being posh about your job. It's the Michael Caine theory about film making: just do it. You know you'll do some turkeys, but you'll do some good ones as well. The other thing is working hard. The one comment in common from all the people I interviewed, when I asked them all the same question – what made them different? – was, more often than not, that they worked harder. They just actually worked harder.

Athletes and sportsmen and women, it goes almost without saying, have to train hard. The brilliant do more than that. Robin Smith, with his father omnipresent on the touchline of the rugby pitch, would be up at dawn practising each and every scenario that he might encounter in a real game.

> As it got light, we would be running up and down the side, and we would be visualizing, looking to the next match and the problems I might encounter. From an early age, I started visualizing the side I would be playing, and who was going to be full back. I played centre. I'd run down the corner and he [his father] would be make me dive into the corner and then say, 'Great try, my boy, great!'

Smith said he was more nervous about speaking to an audience for the Robert Half Interview than about facing the West Indies. He knew he would have put in the effort to face the West Indies: 'I've practised and worked hard at my cricket. I'm a great believer in that if you put the hard work in, things will take care of themselves. I'm a great believer that whatever you do in life, you should do it properly.'

In contrast to Smith, Michael Lynagh was consumed by nerves whatever the game, whether it was in front of 200 people for his Australian university, or thousands for a Saracens match against Newcastle. He had to work to overcome them by a huge effort to focus on each manoeuvre he would have to carry out on the pitch. He learnt that the best way to kill the demons of doubt was to tackle them head on, not avoid them.

> People say we've got to focus, but focus on what? That's the key. Actually, the morning of the [World Cup] final in 1991 is a good story because obviously I was very very nervous. I got as nervous as anybody and actually, that's one of the things that I don't miss about rugby. It didn't matter where it was, I got nervous. How to deal with that? Rather than shutting off, I tended to try to focus on what I had to do and concentrate on that and prepare for it.
>
> Take the morning of the 1991 final. I used to try to do something physical in the morning of matches because I found if you sat around the hotel you just got more and more tense. I've forgotten the name of the hotel but it was on the outskirts of London, and it was a little bit misty. I went out to have a kick in the grounds. Nobody would come out with me so I took my boots and a couple of balls, and rather than running and getting the balls I found a little hill. So I kicked the balls up the hill and then they'd roll back down to me. What I found was that I was actually practising a skill that I was going to be using that afternoon, whereas a lot of people try not to think about what they're going to do. They get scared of it and push it away.

Like Roger Black, who goes into this later, Lynagh believed in visualizing the match and mentally rehearsing moves.

Even though I was very nervous and sometimes I didn't want to think about it, I used to mentally rehearse goal kicks from various parts on the pitch and the moves we were going to do. By 'mentally rehearse', I mean actually lying down and being in a state where I could see gaps opening up on the pitch. I would go through my routine of actually kicking the ball, seeing the referee give a penalty on a certain spot, me placing it, the sand boy coming out and giving me some sand, and so on. All that sort of stuff. So I actually deal with the pressure, deal with the issues, rather than pushing them into the background and trying not to think about them.

Lynagh's preparation included visiting the grounds and practising goal kicks – part of the overall professionalism he says was inculcated in him by the attitude to rugby in Australia even before it turned professional. When he tried it at Twickenham he had to gain permission in advance and undertake not to damage the turf!

When I came here to play for Saracens, because it was professional, I felt the pressure even more. All of a sudden, my ability to put the ball between the posts and win games meant that families, the guys I was playing with, could actually pay the mortgage and eat that week and have bonuses. So there was a new pressure that I had to deal with. I did more practice than I'd ever done before. If we were playing down in Bristol, I'd drive down on my own and actually practise on the pitch the day before. In a way, I became a much better goal kicker than I ever was before because of the time and the pressure that was on me.

The Australian way dictated that every aspect of the game was studied in advance, from the referee to the pitch, and that every possible professional aid was enlisted. They studied the opposition, they studied the referees, they were fit, and they used athletic coaches. It helped to win the World Cup in 1991, but the end-of-tour party was still partly financed by going out on to the streets and selling T-shirts the team had had printed.

Lynagh's technique for that all-elusive focus is simple, although much harder to do. He concentrates on the routine of the task and pushes the possible outcome out of his mind. It's actually a very old-fashioned concept – 'look after the pennies and the pounds will look after themselves', as many of us were told as children – but one rarely used in a professional environment. Yet it makes perfect sense: any major task broken down into its parts is easier to tackle.

Lynagh taught himself to block out everything but the act he had to perform. He learnt to adopt an almost trance-like state.

> It would be down to how I kneeled, how I'd place the ball, the line I'd see from the seam of the ball through the post to the middle and actually which side it was going to hit at the back. Focusing on the outcome often causes failure. Focus on the task in hand and the outcome will look after itself. The ability to be able to do that as a team, as an individual and as a goal kicker is absolutely crucial to performance. If we start worrying about where we are going, what the score is going to be and are we going to win, then forget about it. It's each individual play you do. If you execute that well, then go to the next play, the scoreboard will look after itself.

Athletes concur that the mental aspect is huge in competitive sport. Mental confidence, however, comes through being in good physical shape and ready to do the job. Sebastian Coe says he was always mentally bouncy when he knew he had left no stone unturned in training, and had had a clear run.

> If you're not in good shape, that's when the good poker players really take over. I've gone out on to the line before a race knowing that in reality, the training has gone badly, I've not been in good shape, I've perhaps been injured or whatever. In poker terms, you've just had a handful of crap really, but you've actually got through it because you've kept a mask and people think well, he's as good as he was six months ago. If you don't let them know that you've been injured and that you've been out for a bit, you can normally wing it a bit.

Coe is not totally convinced about the benefits of sports psychologists (unlike Lynagh, whose psychologist father schooled him in 'switching' his brain into slow motion before he kicked for goal). Like Roger Black, who describes later how it took him a decade to find the best mental state, aggressive cassette tapes and high tension did not work for him.

> When I was leaving the sport I'd be warming up in warm-up tracks thinking I was doing all the right things, alongside 18-year-olds who were lying there with Walkmans, with tapes telling them how they were going to destroy the field and how to relax. I was thinking it would be so much easier to just go out and run, actually. The mental side is big and sports psychologists are now part of the circuit. You meet athletes and the first people they introduce you to are their sport psychologists. Some of them are quite weird as well; they have got some very funny ideas about what it is you should be doing. I always found I was mentally at my best when I was physically in good shape.

The mental side of athletics is, as Coe says, 'huge'. Roger Black spent 10 years before he realized that the right mental state for him was total calm. He says that it is possible to learn to be cool under pressure and that will give you the edge – but only provided all other factors are equal.

> You hear lots of people say that in sport, it's 90 per cent in the mind. That's absolute bollocks, I can tell you that. If you're injured, it doesn't matter how strong your mind is. You can be as strong as you want but you're not going to run to the best of your ability. It's 90 per cent in the mind – in fact, it's 100 per cent – as long as you're healthy and the people you're running against are of equal talent to you.

In sport and business, the same tenet applies: leave nothing to chance. Never count on winging it. Nothing makes up for doing homework, groundwork and thorough, all-round preparation.

Nicola Horlick manages to work away from home because she arranges it. 'I'm not nearly as organized as people would like to suggest, but what I am good at is surrounding myself with organized people,' she says. 'I have a very good secretary and good home help and so on. The important thing is to surround yourself with people who are organized, because I can't remember everything.' Part of her effectiveness at work is due to an appreciation of basic organization and effective systems. It is amazing, Horlick says, how frequently these basics are missing.

When she joined Morgan Grenfell, it was in decline, but in five years she and Keith Percy, her colleague, who had built up Phillips and Drew Fund Management, quadrupled it to £22 billion. They did this largely by 'putting in place some basic standards', such as making sure all the secretaries were producing notes in the same format and that there were proper files for the clients. They also combined the research department and the fund managers, a radical management change.

But Horlick's ultimate success depends on winning business. In this, she says, thoroughness is essential. Although her presentation does not change much apart from small evolutions, the facts alter each time. She and her team try to miss nothing: whether the company is British or foreign, private sector or public, who the directors are, who is on the board of trustees and how they relate to the company – and even where the meeting will be, the shape of the room and where the table is. They speak to people in advance so that they know how keen they are to have the business. Horlick says: 'You'd be surprised how few people actually do all those things, so we put a very large emphasis on making sure we are extremely well prepared and that there are no surprises.'

Make sure there are no surprises. Can you do it? You can, even in sport. Roger Black is a believer in visualization, the intelligent assessment of what might and could happen. Most of us never do this in our working lives, although it would present no great challenge. Black says:

> I think if you can anticipate what might happen and see it happening, then if it does happen, it is no surprise to you. You can use it in everyday life. The word visualization makes people think that this is just dreaming, but it has been absolutely proven that your brain cannot tell the difference between something you actually do and something you vividly imagine.

As if to prove his case, he mentions that the hurdler David Hemery, the 1968 400-metre Olympic gold medallist, can actually make himself sick as if he were at the end of a race. Don't try this at home (unless near a bathroom). Black says that the ability to be cool under pressure is part of the same mental mastery.

> The ability to be cool under pressure is something in sport that many people think you've either got or you haven't. The greats, the people like Michael Jordan, the basketball player, he lives for that moment when there are one or two seconds left and he gets the ball and that, for him, is the moment. But other players don't want that because pressure is about the fear of failure. I spent much of my career thinking about what happens if I don't succeed. You have the ability to perform under pressure when you know there is no such thing as failure.

In his own book, Black claims that the harder you try, the slower you go. Relaxation is the secret, and that takes confidence. Confidence comes from being up to the task.

> It takes an enormous amount of confidence to do that because of the people around you. For you to tell yourself to relax is hard. The best example I can think of is Carl Lewis, a 100-metres runner who was always very relaxed. He would come through at the end, not because he was running any faster, but because he would decelerate less. He would give the impression that he was running faster, but he was actually staying more relaxed. That, and pace judgement, are the keys.
>
> I think the secret to any running event, certainly a sprint event, is total relaxation. The ability to have the confidence inwardly to do very little and to hand over to your relaxed body and not push it.

For leading yachtsmen, sponsorship is vital. Once again, research and thoroughness are the keys to begin negotiations. Thus is was that Chay Blyth first captured the imagination (and the funding) of British Steel – by tapping in to its 'steel appeal' campaign and demonstrating how a steel boat would fly the flag for the product. 'It so happened like in all things, timing is critical,' he says. 'They were running a steel appeal campaign, showing the versatility of steel from frocks to shoes, knives and forks to boats. This fitted in very well with the campaign.'

Tony Bullimore expands on the mechanics of fitting a sponsor to the project:

> You need to be able to say a lot and make an impact very quickly and not waffle in a letter, page after page. You have to express your campaign; show how the project can work in synergy with the organization; talk to the right people; lay out why the organization should sponsor you; express who you are and what you're trying to achieve. You certainly have to show where the return is on the sponsor's investment, and it's got to be clear cut.
>
> I try not to be my own presenter. I usually have a couple of people with me; one person would be the spokesperson, who is slightly aloof from what I'm trying to do. Then I don't get so emotional. 'We can do it! We can do it!' is not what an organization want to hear. They want to know what it is you're doing, how it works, how they slot in, what their return is on the investment, are they targeting the right marketplace...and so on. You really have to research the organization that you're trying to draw in as a sponsoring partner. There are organizations I don't bother to go to because there is no synergy. Another organization fits just like a glove – then you have to rapidly prove that.

Chay Blyth's transformation of his own abiding passion into a successful business – enabling other people to share that challenge – is a model of planning and execution, based on his knowledge of the human condition as well as on sound economic calculation. It is also a model of organic growth, with the fleet expanding vessel by vessel and the organization virtually person by person.

> I've always believed that people want adventure and challenges. I was an instructor at an Outward Bound school, having been seconded from the Paras for a short period of time. After I'd sailed round the world, the BSC very generously gave me the boat. That itself is a fantastic thing, but immediately you get the bills for it – insurance, moorings, and the taxman hovering wanting to talk about capital gains. People used to go sailing in the summertime, but not in the winter, so I would find it quite difficult to make an income from getting the boat to work.

When we sold the challenge to British Steel we said the price would be £15,000 or thereabouts. They liked the idea, but couldn't understand that people would pay £15,000 to go round the world on this race. They had a get-out clause that said the launch date was 3 January, but if we hadn't signed up 20 people by 1 October, they could withdraw. In the first week, we'd sold 60 places and in three weeks we were full up. When we launched the BT Global Challenge, we were full up in three days. We've now started the mailing list for the year 2004.

In a youth-obsessed world, Blyth insists that the average age should be 38, which originally came about by accident but which he says gives interest, balance and contrast. 'The young people have no bloody patience at all and want everything tomorrow, and to do this and that. The older people say, "What about this? Let's do a bit more that." They've got something to bring to the party. It's really quite interesting, especially the conflict.'

Blyth's application and thoroughness are hugely effective at getting sponsors on board, for which he is renowned.

The key, first and foremost, is that the company has to understand what its objectives are. Once it's done that, we have to try to mould what we have to offer to fit those objectives. No two companies have the same contract. Timing also plays an important part and generally, we allow 12 months from the day of contact through to completion. For Rover, it took two-and-a-half years. Companies, if they're forced to a decision, invariably say 'no'. So we never, ever push for one. We just have to wait patiently.

He also remains extraordinarily focused, so that ordinary human weaknesses – loneliness at sea, self-doubt, fear – are kept at bay.

I sit down and write the project. I put down the aim of the exercise, the objectives, all the facts involved, all the bits and pieces, and at the end of the day come up with a conclusion. The conclusion is that you're either going to run with the project, or run with it so far to see if it's going to be viable, or whatever. At the end of the day you have a conclusion. If the conclusion is 'yes', it's what you've got to get out there and do… Certainly, on the British Steel Challenge, I tried to maintain as much discipline on a daily basis as possible – three meals a day, an all-over wash and shave every Sunday, regardless of the weather. It'd be freezing bloody cold, but I still did it. Focus is the name of the game.

There is a degree of detachment about Blyth's style. There is also a determination (which he shares with Ken Bates) to keep major plans under wraps.

The mistake I wouldn't make is exactly the one that Johnson and Hoare made [when they announced they were going to row across the Atlantic, and were beaten by Blyth and Ridgeway]. We, as a company, keep everything secret. When anyone comes for induction, the first thing they're told is that what is our business is our business, and stays our business. Any new projects, we give an exercise name to, and we never discuss it outside the office. It's kept close tabs until we're ready to launch. That's the lesson I learnt from them. It's great – it's like being in the SAS!

Ken Bates says this about running a business well out of the spotlight:

You don't go after players in the press. Firstly you upset the club you want to get the player from, which means they'll sell him to somebody else rather than you, or they jack the price up. Secondly you bring in competition, which can jack up the price again. Thirdly you upset your existing players. Chelsea – apart from one mistake – doesn't talk about what it's going to do; it just does it.

Bates displays the same detached pragmatism and ability to think laterally. Chelsea's ground cannot accommodate more than 41,000 seats because of planning regulations so, as Bates says, other sources of income had to be found.

The first need was to jack the prices up: that's why we are the most expensive club in the country. Then there were six acres of land not used for anything. Now we have a hotel. When we finish we'll have a hotel, nine restaurants, sports and leisure centre, night clubs, a business centre and banqueting suite, 10–15 conference rooms and an exhibition hall. There will also be another hotel, a megastore, an underground car park and another 3,000 square feet of retailing space. The City has a phrase called 'sweating the assets'. By the time we've finished, sweat will be coming out of every pore at Chelsea.

Every department at Chelsea is a profit centre, including football (although it is the core business). Buying players, says Bates, is 'no more difficult in a business sense than head hunting. Some turn out to be good and some turn out to be duck eggs. We sit down and discuss the requirements of the team … you have a budget and then you have to plan accordingly. If it's not within the budget you don't do it.'

There is an interesting balance between the desire to do a job well and the necessity to remember that, however grand the passion, it still has to work as a business. Harvey Goldsmith discovered this early – very early, during the hippy era.

I admired the hippy side of things, but decided that if I was to survive in this business, I couldn't participate with them. I felt I had some kind of empathy towards musicians and other people behind the scenes. I had this innate organizational ability and I didn't know it at the time, but an eye for talent. If I've joined them, and if ever there was a problem, I had to think how I got myself out and how I got them out of the mess. So I decided that they were enjoying it their way, and I'd enjoy it my way, and I'd take one step back.

For me, it's worked very well. You can get close to some artists and some of them obviously become great friends as you work with them year after year – but it's still a client–business relationship. We are dealing with people all the time, and people change their minds and have different influences put upon them. There's always someone who's jealous and who will try to get at you and so forth. You feel you're part of the club, but to actually survive you keep one step away from it, and have some understanding of when to say, I've hung out long enough, I need to keep back.

We end this chapter on hard work, application, detachment and (in the final analysis) bottom lines, with Raymond Blanc. Anyone who has ever worked in a kitchen will tell you: catering is hellishly hard. And that's just serving up chips. When the cuisine is haute and you aspire to be the best, then the heat is really white hot.

> You are putting these little meaningless details together day after day, year after year; success is an act of will. It just does not happen. You don't dream about success, you make it happen every day. All these millions of little details, you pile them up together until you have density, volume and then you are close to excellence.
>
> Many people often make the mistake of comparing cuisine *de grande mere* and *haute cuisine*. They simply do not compare for they are not comparable. You would not compare Agatha Christie or Lord Archer's writing with Dostoevsky or Oscar Wilde. They simply don't compare. One appeals to simple enjoyment and instant gratification. Both intellect and sensitivities do not have to be that present. It is a plainly enjoyable gutsy book to read, in a very simple form. The other one needs complete attention because there are so many sensitivities and undertones in every sentence; in the way it is constructed. The plot is far more meaningful. There is a far deeper study of each personality and each character. This is the difference between a pleasing and enjoyable novel and literature.
>
> My mother's cuisine is just that. It appeals to the appetite, it is delicious, it is wholesome; you don't have to think about it. It is fresh from the garden and she applies her simple craft and puts it on to a table. *Haute cuisine* is entirely different. There you are talking about layers and layers of tremendous amounts of details and thoughts that will create lengthy and refined flavours with succession of undertones. Of course the produce is the purest and the noblest. The creative process is never encumbered by untruth or the search for creating effect; creating something new for the sake of it. Then the magic happens. Then food takes the shape of one of the greatest art forms.

4 Team spirit – those without whom it wouldn't have happened

Utterly alone in the cold water of the Southern Ocean, doggedly resisting the temptation to consider the possibility – indeed, the probability – that he would die, Tony Bullimore's solitude had never been more petrifying. Single-handed sailors have to be suited by temperament to spending long periods of time on their own, but brilliant careers are rarely the product of a solo effort.

Most of our subjects have had help along the way. Some have had the sort of involved and practical support without which their careers would not have taken off at all. Others have had less active, but constant support from parents and wives (and husbands). Most have looked to inspirational figures – heroes, sometimes – to provide guidance and reinforcement.

Brilliant careers are often a bit like icebergs: only a very small part shows on the surface, but the support foundations are considerably bigger. For every hero out at sea, there is a support team in the background keeping the ordinary business of life afloat. For every high-flying business person, there is usually an unseen *domestique* keeping normal life ticking.

The desire to be part of a team, even its leader, is part of the normal human condition. The sum of the effort of several is greater than several separate campaigns.

It took Tony Bullimore a long time to get to grips with this. His constant background support has come from his wife, Lalel, to whom he has been married for more than 35 years. After his rescue from the Southern Ocean, he promised her that she would have to give him written permission to sail again. 'She turned round and said, "I can't stop you doing what you do, it's gone on too long." My wife respects the fact that this is what I do, it's my way of life.' His longer-term plans involve selling their house in Bristol, buying a small apartment and acquiring a cottage in Jamaica, where Lalel was born. Without her compliance, he could not have pursued his passion for the sea (or gained the accolade of Yachtsman of the Year in 1985, when he won 28 races throughout Europe).

Later in life, Bullimore was enjoying working with others (and had also found a respect for professions he once dismissed). Asked how important support and recognition from others has been in maintaining purpose and enthusiasm, he replied:

> Extremely important. One of my failures in the early part of my life was that I was very much a loner, a bit of a one-man band. I wasn't a good team man in my business. I was the one who made all the decisions. In the early days, whether it was my accountants, my lawyers, my bankers, other people with a lot of experience in different situations, I had to set to pace. I don't think it did me too much good. Some people have admired me for my one-man-band attitude of 'let's go out there and beat the drum and go for it'. But I think most people didn't see that as a very good quality.
>
> As the years rolled by, I gradually became more accustomed to being with other people. It was a long time ago that I became a team man. I developed into that and I think the only way I will go forward now is to work with other people.

Chay Blyth, our other yachtsman, has been in a unique position to observe the dynamics of team working, not only as the organizer of the BT Global Challenge round-the-world event, but as the instigator of a rowing race from Cannes to Barbados. Thirty teams went. Blyth has concluded that personality clashes and difficulties can be overcome, but only provided the focus of the effort remains clear, and the motivation strong enough to overcome human frailties. By the end of the rowing race, in which 30 teams participated, some were not even on speaking terms.

His perceptions are not only objective: in 1966, as a sergeant in the Parachute Regiment, he and Captain John Ridgeway broke the record for rowing across the Atlantic, completing 3,000 miles in 92 days. 'There is no such thing as equality in the services,' Blyth observes. In campaigns where it is necessary for some to take orders and some to give them, he adds, this is an advantage.

> In some ways it worked extremely well, because John had some experience in the sailing or boating world, because he'd been educated at a nautical college. He was a captain, therefore he was used to giving orders. I was a sergeant and I was used to taking orders. I was much more practical than John was. John would come in and do the airy-fairy bit and then disappear, and I'd get down to the practicalities. When it divided into responsibility, he'd take all the things such as navigation and seamanship. I would take over radio, survival, equipment, food, medical, that sort of thing. It worked very well.

Blyth and Ridgeway were assisted by force of habit: as Paras, they were used to tremendous physical effort and discipline. They were also used to rowing two hours on and two hours off throughout the night (they rowed together for the other 12 hours).

> You have to be a bit careful about who you take – you have to decide what the focus is. The two people who won [the rowing race] were Kiwis, and they were very very focused indeed. They entered the next race as well, but not together. Clearly, they don't get on that well with each other now, but because they're so focused and the end product is what it's all about, they would put up with that, the same as John and I did in a lot of ways. In three months [together] you're not going to get it all right, but we had a rule that we didn't criticize anything that happened on the boat. We kept it to ourselves until 25 years had passed. Our focus was to finish.

For his inspiration to sail – and to turn his sport into a business, Blyth looked to Sir Francis Chichester.

Sir Francis Chichester laid down the foundations. He is really the daddy of all sponsorship in terms of sailing, a brilliant character. He gave the impression that he wasn't sponsored at all, but in fact he was sponsored up to the eyeballs. He'd gone round the world one-stop and clearly somebody was going to do it non-stop. A whole gamut of people wanted to do that.

Robin Smith has already described the passion with which his father propelled him to sporting success. Smith's career is populated by those he has seen as being on his side. He has loved being among the characters of cricket, such as Ian Botham and Alan Lamb. His heroes share the quality he most admires: calmness under pressure.

I admire Freddie Couples, the golfer, for his temperament, his smiling, relaxed and courteous manner, his time for people. I admire Stefan Edberg playing tennis – he is calm under pressure – and Michael Jordan, the basketball player.

Behind Smith for 12 years has been his wife, Kath – 'I certainly think being married for 12 years is an achievement , specially for my wife, putting up with me' he says. Kath Smith broke her usual silence in 1998, when her husband was surprisingly left out of the England side, writing to the chairman of the England selectors, David Graveney. Her letter was published in the *Mail on Sunday*:

I am so angry about the rough justice you appear to have dealt my husband's cricket career…Something must be drastically wrong when Robin is allowed to play silly cricket in St Moritz at the same time as England's batsmen are falling on their swords in a Test in Trinidad. It has broken my heart this winter when Robin has been stopped in the streets and asked, 'Why aren't you in the West Indies showing England how to bat against those fast bowlers?' Robin is still good enough and should be out there because his record shows that when England are up against it, there is no better man for a crisis.

Chris Smith, Robin's elder brother, provided the right balance between encouragement and chastisement.

He's a real workaholic. During his cricket career he worked a lot harder than anybody else. Having said that, talent only gets you 20 per cent of the way, and maybe I would rather have his qualities in life more than just having talent on the cricket field. He is far more successful than I am now, and good luck to him. He is a great bloke and has been a fantastic influence on my career. He has encouraged me – and has actually been very hard on me.

I'm one of those people who are naturally lazy and need a kick up the bum every now and then. By the same token, I also need a good pat on the back and to be encouraged. He has the balance right, and had it not been for his guidance and encouragement through my early days, and also through my career at Hampshire until he retired five years ago, I don't think I would have been half the player I was.

Smith's colleagues have made his career a pleasure.

Only when you retire and look back do you realize how special it was, and what a great privilege. When you have to get into the real world and work hard for a living, you appreciate what a great time you had playing for England. With regard to the party animals – Beefy [Ian Botham] and Lamby [Alan Lamb] are just awesome. You get a great team spirit, a great camaraderie. It's a wonderful experience with some great characters. Unfortunately there aren't as many characters now as there were in the past because they try to stamp it out, which is a real shame. Characters bring excitement to the game.

For the principal dynamo in the Smith career, however, we have to look close to home again, and to Smith *père*. In any case, there are anecdotes relating to the estimable John Smith that should not be omitted. Here is his son on the lengths to which his father has, at various times, been willing to go and, indeed, still goes:

I love my dad to bits but he is definitely a couple of bottles short of a crate – the bloke is in a different division. He has probably watched 80 per cent of my cricketing days for 19 years, all around the country and all round the world. He's there all the time; he sits there with his bottle of scotch and his packet of fags, with his music on, and he is absolutely besotted by cricket. Some people say maybe he put pressure on me. Maybe he did, but I wouldn't change it for the world.

We used to go down in the rugby season to the school I went to. It was right on the water, and when the sun was beginning to set, all I could see was a silhouette of an upright post. I used to get a ball and he used to sit under the post with a great big lantern, so I could actually aim for the lantern. I would kick the ball, and if it landed about 10 or 15 yards away, he would say, 'Robin my boy, follow through properly, how many times must I tell you?' I would put it back down, follow it through properly – and just occasionally I'd hit the rugby ball right in the middle. I'd think, 'That's a good shot', and all of a sudden – bang! – the light would go out. Dad would get up, switch on the light, and go 'Good kick my boy!'

Towards the end of the season, we played a game on a very wet and windy Saturday afternoon. It was a local derby and there were 4,000 people there. On one side there was a great big pavilion where everybody was sitting and on the other side there was just my dad, the coach and the linesman. The coach was never really allowed to encourage the players because he had been told off by the headmaster, so the coach would get my dad to come and encourage the players and give out the instructions.

On this occasion, we had been unbeaten all season, and so had the team down the road. In the dying moments of the game we were about three points behind and I got the ball within the 10-yard line and as I got it, I nudged over the other centre and ran towards the fullback. Just out of the corner of my eye I saw my dad just starting to develop a bit of speed on the line, and there he was in white trousers, white socks, white shoes and a white shirt. As I was gathering speed, the fullback came up to me and I shoved a hand in his face and he went down, and as I did that, I saw my dad do the same thing to the linesman! He just collapsed in a heap.

Here I was running down, I was now only two yards from my old man, he was running with me and as I dived in the corner so did he. It was raining, and we ended up in a heap. I looked up and I thought, 'Oh no.' I had a girlfriend who had come for the first time to see me play and she was sitting with my mum. She was so embarrassed that she got up and walked off and I never saw her again, unfortunately. She said 'I am certainly not having a father-in-law like that in my life!'

That's my dad. He's a tremendous character and such a great bloke. All the success I have had in my life is really down to the sheer enjoyment, passion, determination and encouragement that he gave me. He's brilliant.

Two other fathers who have played outstanding roles in their children's careers are Peter Coe, father of Sebastian, and Ian Lynagh, father of Michael. Coe's father is an engineer who used engineering principles to coach athletics, while Lynagh's father is a psychologist who used his profession to exert an enormous influence on his career.

In 1984, I was selected in the Grand Slam Test teams. We had beaten England by 19-3 at Twickenham in the first game. I kicked a total of about three out of nine, then we went to Ireland and once again I kicked badly. For the Welsh Test I was dropped from the goal kicking. I was left in the team but Roger Gould did the goal kicking – the only Test in my career in which I didn't goal kick. Then there was the Scottish Test, and the day before, the coach, Alan Jones, said that Roger Gould and I were doing the kicking. I couldn't miss anything at training while Roger was digging up turf, spraying it everywhere, a bit like my golf!

[Before the Scottish Test] I had worked with my father. What we had found was that because I was playing inside centre rather than fly half, and it was a much more physical position, my arousal level was a lot higher. Therefore, when it came to doing a fine motor skill like goal kicking I couldn't do it. It's a bit like asking Greg Norman to tee off, pick up his clubs and run to the next one, pushing off a bit of the gallery here and there, then make a couple of tackles on a few press photographers, hit a five iron to the green and do the same thing again and then sink a 10-foot putt. That's what I liken goal kicking to. It's a very useful analogy.

Because my arousal level was so high, due to the fact that I was in a more forceful position, the radar was just a little bit out. What we did for the Scottish Test was come up with a little plan. As soon as I was to goal kick, I would mentally push the slow motion button on my brain. So everything – from the breathing to getting the ball to getting the sand from the guy – was done in slow motion. It was normal speed to anybody who was looking. By bringing everything down to a slower level it enabled me to execute a fine motor skill. I kicked eight out of nine that day, an Australian record, and we won the Grand Slam. There were examples like that all through my career of how my father helped, and this was before sports psychology became fashionable. It was certainly helpful to me.

It is perhaps in sport that the value of mentors and role models is most clearly seen (although it is not necessarily more significant than in other walks of life). As Roger Black explains later, just one remark or piece of advice can endure for ever. In Lynagh's case, one of these potent maxims came from his school headmaster, Brother Buckley, a keen sportsman. Lynagh was captain of the first XI cricket team when Buckley, a great cricket supporter, came to watch and saw him win the toss.

I won the toss and I said we'd bat. I was walking back and Brother Buckley asked me, 'What did you do?' I said, 'I chose to bat, but I don't really know.' He said to me – and I've never forgotten this – 'You've made the decision, now what you have to do is make that decision work.' I thought it's so simple, but he's right. The decision is irrelevant; the only way you can affect the result now is going and scoring a few runs. That was a lesson I kept in my mind. You make the decision and go and make it work, have confidence.

Sebastian Coe, whose expert coaching by his father gave them a different relationship from their otherwise conventional one, corroborates what Lynagh has to say about the value of coaching (which, Lynagh also says, is taken more seriously in Australia, where young talent is spotted and nurtured: if the UK wants to achieve sporting excellence, it should put money into coaching).

Coe says: 'No athlete makes it to the top, whether they are a rower or a tennis player, without good coaches that are well resourced. I do feel very strongly about this and would like to see more consideration given within the Lottery funding structure for coaching.'

Coe did have an excellent coach without looking for one: his father. He referred to his father as Peter, and his father referred to him as 'my athlete', alongside the three or four other athletes he was coaching at the time.

Ken Bates

Roger Black

Raymond Blanc

Chay Blyth

Tony Bullimore

Sebastian Coe

Harvey Goldsmith

Nicola Horlick

Michael Lynagh

Michael Parkinson

Tony Robinson

Robin Smith

Nicola Horlick

Raymond Blanc

Robin Smith

Michael Parkinson

Roger Black

Tony Bullimore

Michael Lynagh

Roger Black

Harvey Goldsmith

Sebastian Coe

Chay Blyth

The press used to think this was really quite odd. We were able to deal with that a lot easier than they were. The one rule we always had was we would never allow a family issue, which inevitably there are from time to time, to spill over on to the training track, and we would never take the training track back to the supper table.

There are probably more pressures if it is a father–son relationship. A coach–athlete relationship is probably the closest relationship you are ever going to have with somebody outside of a marriage, and it's equally volatile on occasions. When you're coached by a relative, there are pressures on the rest of the family. I have four other brothers and sisters and so organizing a family around my training and having the balance in the family so that there isn't a focus just on one kid in the family was very important. My mother was very instrumental in making sure there was equilibrium for the family, which could very easily have tilted far too far in one direction.

His father, Coe says, was far in advance of his time, recruiting a physiologist in 1983, who worked with Coe until the end of his career. Peter Coe had his son's diet balanced by a nutritionist from his son's old university, Loughborough, and recruited a biomechanics expert from Leeds University. Coe says:

What my dad did was put together the first management team in athletics, which is now commonplace. The only thing he didn't have much time for was the sports psychologist. He brought this team together and then set the schedules. Setting training schedules is the job of the coach. Coaches need to have the discipline and the specialist knowledge that informs their judgement, then they put the programme together.

Coe has taken influences from 'lots' of heroes, including Muhammad Ali. 'I think anybody who grew up during his career would choose him, as well as people who didn't. I have kids down at my athletic club who are a quarter of my age who would give you the same answer. The impact he had on the sporting 20th century was mammoth.' From his own sport, Coe took inspiration from Brendan Foster.

I was brought up in the north of England and Brendan had quite a large impact, in that he was the first athlete within my frame of reference who could be seen winning major titles overseas. It was a relative rarity. My athletic career basically started in the early 1970s and by the early 1980s we still hadn't got anybody who was consistently winning championships overseas. Brendan was the first of that breed. He broke world records; you could switch a television on and Brendan was the equal of any of the Kenyans – and some of those dreaded East Germans we only read about in cartoons.

Raymond Blanc also returns to his roots for his biggest influence: his parents. 'They gave me that knowledge of food. I would also say the modern masters of French cuisine like Guerard, who first moved away from Escoffier and on to modern French cuisine.'

Although he prides himself on being self-taught, and on the independent spirits of his protégés, Blanc acknowledges other cohorts in the campaign to change the British hands-off attitude to food and to make it the preserve of everyone and not, as he sees it, the *bourgeoisie*. Delia Smith, he says, has done more for cooking and the popularity of cooking than any other food writer, including Mrs Beaton and Elizabeth David.

They are great ladies in their own right, with great knowledge, but made food the allegiance of the rich and the ruling classes. They didn't popularize it. They strengthened the status of food as being a bourgeois occupation and for the rich. Delia Smith has done a fantastic job, and other celebrity chefs as well, in spreading the word that food is fun. So I think bravo! Maybe her form of expression is not elaborate or sophisticated, but she has done a fantastic job.

Michael Parkinson once admitted, years on, that he had actually been jealous of his wife Mary's success as a TV host – because her considerable talents had found another outlet. He had regarded her as his rock. The couple, who married in 1959, when Parkinson was a local newspaper reporter in Doncaster and Mary a secondary modern school teacher, have three grown-up sons, and grandchildren. 'I'm never bored by her,' he says. 'I can't contemplate life without Mary.'

We thought I might become news editor of the _Yorkshire Post_ and Mary might become a headmistress. Then all of a sudden I moved to Fleet Street and then Granada Television and my career started to take off. It put an enormous strain on Mary, who was left behind. It was then I learned the marvellous truth about her: that she was this gutsy and adaptable person who was basically fearless. It was because of her that we made this extraordinary journey from Doncaster to here, and made it without too much compromise about who we are, without breaking up, and rearing a family at the same time. That's been my real achievement. The rest, the professional stuff, doesn't really matter.

Parkinson disclosed how much he still depends on his wife in an interview with Brian Reade in _The Mirror_ two years ago:

For the first time in my life I'm frightened. I am starting to think morbid things, even though we are both healthy, touch wood. It's not that I might die, but that she might. We have been so happy together and now suddenly I am getting this awful dread about losing her. The realization has dawned that one day one of us won't be there. Over the years we have become like one person, indispensable to each other. If there is anything that's irreplaceable in my life, it's her. There just wouldn't be enough time left for me to find a similar relationship, even if I had the inclination. I don't honestly know how or why it's lasted, I just thank God that it has. For all the possibilities that there were to walk away in the past 40 years – and there were possibilities – we didn't.

Nicola Horlick's husband, Tim, was behind her when she flew to Frankfurt to confront her bosses at Deutsche Bank about her suspension: 'He wasn't sure it was necessarily the right thing to have done, but I'm very fortunate in that he was always very supportive through the whole thing, mainly because he knew it was unfair. He didn't criticize me in any way.'

Horlick's domestic circumstances, as a wife and mother of six children, one of whom died, have meant she has relied heavily on a support system.

The children must come first. They are the most important thing. As it happens it seems to have worked out because I have had good child-care, the support of a very helpful and young mother. I have my brother living near me and he is very helpful. I have had a lot of support around me, and supportive colleagues.

Horlick has borrowed freely for her modus operandi from role models at work. She names Leonard Licht, the Vice Chairman of SG Warburg & Co when she joined in 1983, and the best-known woman fund-manager of all, Carol Galley.

Leonard used to say, 'Always sell on the first profits warning, because there are bound to be more coming behind it.' He was a very decisive person; that's where I learnt it was good to be decisive. He was probably the best fund manager in the City during the 1970s, 1980s and probably the early 1990s as well. Carol Galley is an incredibly organized person, the person who put the discipline into the business. Leonard was the sort of artist, and Carol was more the scientist. All the meticulous writing of notes which I have always believed is very important – not just notes of meetings which you have been to with clients, but also preparing well for company meetings, making sure you write up the meetings afterwards – all that I learnt from Carol.

Roger Black now runs a motivational business and through his long career absorbed a wealth of information about motivation. In his view, other people are not just aids to excellence, but components. Black's views suggest that it is almost impossible to be brilliant in total isolation. Other people's experiences – good as well as bad – have been incorporated into Black's career.

People often ask me what is the most important thing about training: is it a great coach? No. The most important things are your training partners, the people with whom you surround yourself every day, with whom you share the same goals, the same dreams and the same aspirations. Especially if you're thinking about being the best in the world, it helps to have somebody around you who is also trying to be the best in the world. I was lucky because my training partner for the first half of my career was Kriss Akabusi. He is great fun to have around and such a great example – behind that jovial person is somebody who is so focused, so dedicated, so disciplined.

If Tony Robinson is 'like blotting paper' for knowledge, Roger Black has adopted that principle for his own motivation. He takes motivation from everything – from books written for that purpose, to brief conversations that are otherwise unrelated. He has been inspired by novels – and even by the lyrics of songs. He says: 'When I have conversations with people, I am looking for something that can make a difference to my life. When I read certain books I don't think I have to get all of it, just one piece of information.'

> Some of the most motivational books I have read have been novels and biographies. _The Evil Cradling_ by Brian Keenan, the hostage, had a major impact on me. I was feeling really sorry for myself because I had glandular fever. Then I read his book about his five years in captivity and how he managed to maintain his identity, and it put everything into perspective for me.
>
> From the motivational point of view, the biggest influence on me has been a guy in America, Tony Robbins, who is a big motivational person, both literally and metaphorically. The Steven Covey book _The Seven Habits of Highly Successful People_, is great.
>
> Lyrics of songs also inspire me. I listened to certain songs before I ran, and some of them were really motivating for me, although they weren't written for those reasons. The most important was a line in a song sung by the band Aztec Camera, written by Roddy Frame. He wrote a lyric that really crystallized things for me: 'The secret is silver, it's to shine and to never simply survive.'

Most surprisingly, Black points out that other people's failures are useful in building your own career. One of his mentors was David Jenkins, a 400-metres runner in the 1970s and world number one for a year. Jenkins, however, always underperformed in championships and despite his brilliance never won an Olympic medal. Instead, he turned to steroids, and after retirement became a drug trafficker in San Diego. He was caught and sent to prison. Black had known him in California, where he used to train for three months of the year.

In 1995 I felt I needed a bit of guidance, and it could only come from somebody who had been in the same position and had messed up. I often think you can learn more from people who have tried to do what you do and failed – you can learn as much from them as from people who have tried and succeeded. I asked Jenkins to help me and he changed my way of thinking.

He asked me in 1996 what my goals were. I had been taught you must have very clear goals and must write them down, which I think is true. I had a performance goal and an outcome goal. They were pretty good, but he told me to put them to one side. He said from then on, I should have just one goal, but a very simple goal. It's the most effective goal anyone can have. He said, 'I want you to carry it with you on the track when you are training, I want you to carry it with you in competition, but more importantly, I want you to carry it with you off the track: it is to focus on running the perfect race.'

I asked what he meant, and he said to focus on running the perfect race and on nothing else. It seems an obvious thing to me now but at the time, I remember sitting there and thinking, 'God, he's right!' He said he had spent his whole career worrying about what might happen. He said, 'Don't over-analyse it, just enjoy it and do the best you can, and really focus on that.'

That is all I did. A weight came off my shoulders and I began to realize that if I didn't do well at the Olympics it wouldn't be the end of the world. I just became focused on running a 400-metres race as fast as I possibly could. It was the best advice I have ever had.

So far, so good. But let's go to Tony Robinson for a bit of light relief, a glimpse behind the curtain in the world of theatrical egos and temperament. A production, according to Robinson, is a triumph of team spirit over ego. In his experience, this delicate balance can only be maintained for so long. Hence, he says, the comparative brevity of some of the most brilliant shows (even if the holders of the careers involved move on to achieve this successful but short-lived balance elsewhere). The more the equality of status, Robinson says, the more that tension struggles to rise to the surface.

When you start a series like that, most people involved are pretty egotistical and have a whole series of different visions but actually, they are prepared to sacrifice an awful lot of that for the good of the whole. The more the series goes on, and the more successful it gets, the more those contradictions rise to the surface. _Monty Python_ was probably the only really splendid show that went to five series, and even that went to number five without John Cleese. In _Not The Nine O' Clock News_, I believe I'm right in saying that outside the rehearsal rooms people were only talking to each other via their solicitor by their fourth series! Very ambitious and talented people get together and squabble.

The problem with the _Adder_ was that Richard [Curtis] and Ben [Elton] would write the stuff and then we would all go away and we would rework it. Understandably, although I think to a certain extent Richard and Ben were very grateful for the way we improved the gags, the fact is we would often go too far, we would alter the plot lines. They would sometimes come back and we would have cast different people in it, we would create new characters. They would get very upset and at the end of each series we said, 'Don't worry, next series we'll make it better, we realize we've given you a hard time, we won't next time.' Each series we made it worse and at the end of the fourth series the two writers walked away from it and said never again!

But Michael Lynagh must have the parting shot about other people.

It's hard for me to explain sitting up here having played all those Tests, but I do see myself as lucky. I'm lucky – very lucky – to have some natural gifts, which I honed and had some confidence to go and use. The one thing I really am a stickler for is this: just because I've done all that, it doesn't mean I have to be a nasty person, or not talk to people, or not give the time of day to people. That for me is the key to being a success: you can have all that but life goes on, and that means nothing unless you let other people enjoy it as well.

Other people

Maurice Saatchi (now Lord Saatchi) is not one of our subjects, despite his brilliant career. But it is interesting to take note of an interview with him this year on success second time round with M&C Saatchi, the Saatchi brothers' successor to Saatchi & Saatchi. Darius Sanai, *The Independent*'s writer, places his subject in 'a large, open-plan office'. The opening observation from Saatchi is this: 'I would never go back to being in an office on my own. If you'd asked me [10 years ago] would I like to work in an open-plan office, I'd have said it was absolutely out of the question.' Now, Saatchi's desk, white with a black leather chair, is distinguished not by its location behind a nameplated door, but by a pile of hardback books.

Successful management has changed dramatically over the past decade, although perhaps more in physical terms than in spiritual. The best managers have always been part of their team rather than external strategists. Saatchi's observation is that collective offices are 'much more alive and energetic'. Nicola Horlick's view is that preserving status-based hierarchies is no way to get the best out of other people.

Brilliant careers are made not only from leaning on and learning from others, but from learning to collaborate and direct in the most effective way. Good managers will always keep an eye on the people they manage, and not just focus on their own plans and goals.

Nicola Horlick inhabits the world of fund management, where collaborative working is so valuable that entire teams can be poached *en masse*. Somewhat controversially, she says that one major bar to effective management is the male ego.

I don't want to be rude about men, but lots of men have big egos, which get in the way. That's not necessarily a trait which women have to the same extent. One of the things that drives me insane in some of these big organizations is that people are told their objectives for the year and then are not spoken to again for another year. At the end of the year, they're told they haven't done very well and their bonus is being cut – and that's the first they've heard of it. That, in my view, is absolutely outrageous, and should never happen. Management is not a twice-a-year thing, but constantly talking to people about what they want to achieve and how they are going to achieve it and if there is a problem, helping them through it.

Horlick also believes that pay differentials for people doing the same job at the same level are not just divisive and damaging to morale, but demotivating.

You should be paying people who are contributing to a team on the same level the same amount. If one is struggling, you should help them to get up to the standard you require. People always find out about £2,000 differences and it completely demotivates them. I can't see that's the right way to manage a business. No one has ever taught me any of this; it's just my instinct tells me that this is the right way to manage a team.

Horlick exploits the feminine side of her personality to get the best out of her team. Bullying and intimidation, she says, are counterproductive. Asked if she is hard nosed, bossy and forceful, she replies that all successful women in business attract those stereotypical adjectives.

That is the 1980s idea of what a successful businesswoman would be like and it's a stereotype that people like to apply to any successful businesswoman. I personally don't recognize that as being me. It's certainly not what successful women in the 1990s are trying to do. The power suits have gone out of the window; the harsh approach and bullying people and all that have gone out of the window. One thing I am absolutely sure of is that if women use the feminine side of their personality in a management sense – ie, the maternal, nurturing aspect

– that they will do very well. It is a very good trait to have when you are trying to build a team. The business I'm in is a team-based business, and I have never emphasized the masculine side of my personality. I think if you are interested in what people want to do and you ask them about what they want to achieve, and encourage them – which are all female ways of doing things – they respond very well to that.

Management through nurturing people certainly works a great deal better than management through fear. You might have a whole load of people who sit there in a very orderly way and look as though they're achieving a lot if you have management through fear. People have to spend an awful long time at work, and do they really want to come to work every day and feel unhappy about it? You want to create an atmosphere where people actually enjoy it and want to be there. If you can do that, and give people the opportunity to climb up the ladder relatively fast – which in the City is very important, because it's a young person's business generally – you end up with a happy and fulfilled team of people, and you also earn their loyalty. I have a very strong view that you can expect people to be committed because you are paying them, but you earn their loyalty.

In Horlick's view, open-plan offices are part of the effective communication, which works best in motivating other people and in getting them to do their best work.

Sitting in open plan is important. It is very tempting when you become senior to go and hide in an office somewhere. That's a big mistake. Even our chief executive sits outside his office, and then the office is just like a little meeting room behind him that he can go into to discuss confidential matters. Everybody sits in open-plan offices and that gives the feeling of total access, for anybody to come up and ask what they want to ask.

We do quarterly staff presentations and we have lunches every month, where we sit down round a table and anybody can ask me anything about anything and I will answer, within reason. I think it's important that there isn't some sort of hierarchy within the organization that keeps all the information to itself. There is a tendency when people are in senior management to be secretive, almost like a power kick. The only reason for it is to make themselves feel important, not because it's necessary. The only thing that should be completely secret is the absolute minute details of remuneration to each individual. Breaking down the idea that we hold all the secrets, and no one else is allowed to know them, is important to pushing forward the idea that it's a flat structure and not a hierarchy.

Responsibility is important. Horlick's performance in management was absolutely tested when she was offered the chance to start a new fund-management organisation, Société Général (SG Asset Management) from scratch. She had already had a similar experience when she and a colleague, Keith Percy, were parachuted into ailing Morgan Grenfell. They started by reorganizing the office and combining the research department and the fund managers. Horlick says: 'The key thing, obviously, was to motivate the team and encourage them. Almost from the moment we reorganized it and gave the younger people who had been in the research department some responsibility, the performance figures turned.'

No amount of philosophical management will make up for recruiting unsuitable people in the first place, however. Horlick recognizes that a certain disposition is more likely to succeed in her business. She looks for people who are decisive and to the point.

Communication is also important, because we have to sit down with a large number of trustees and tell them what we're doing. It's not just a matter of sitting in the office and managing the money; it's also a matter of actually telling them how we are going about it...I look for people who have done a bit of debating or drama, people who aren't afraid to stand up and speak for themselves, because even our morning meetings can be a bit daunting. You're sitting around a table with 12 people, who are very well informed, and you're going to start talking about something they probably know more about than you, and you can be pounced on and shredded.

A flat structure that offers people opportunities to make their mark – and a share in the equity, even better – has no difficulty in attracting potential recruits. When it was announced at the beginning of May 1997 that SG Asset Management and Horlick were in business, the office was deluged. Horlick says: 'I got 600 unsolicited CVs. A lot of the people I employed came via that route, direct. One of them came from a Japanese fund manager who sent his CV over by motorbike courier with the news that he was going back to Japan in four hours.' She interviewed him with colleagues that morning and offered him a job.

> You can do that if you're new, and you've got the resource there. You don't have to go through 18 layers of management to make decisions. We got some incredibly good people just applying direct, who hadn't applied anywhere else. They weren't even necessarily thinking of leaving prior to reading about this. I suppose it just caught people's imagination really. They thought it was all a bit boring, working for very big firms, and the idea of doing something literally from scratch, getting in on the ground floor – and there was equity on offer as well, which was unusual – was too great an opportunity to miss.

From the fevered chic of London fund managers to the greensward of Hampshire Cricket Club is a quantum leap – but not, necessarily, in terms of management. Openness, communication and valuing people are all qualities that Horlick uses in her open-plan office and Robin Smith, Hampshire captain, uses in the dressing room. It is fascinating that Smith has learnt what works not from any management manual but from observing, from his own experience, the techniques that patently do not. The nadir of his career was being dropped from the England team after a successful season in 1998. He criticized the lack of openness and honesty with which he perceived the process had been carried out. He says: 'The main thing I've learnt, having played for England over an eight-year period, was that the managers' management of people was absolutely dreadful. The way I try to operate my captaincy is to do everything the opposite of what they did.'

The rules of thumb, Smith says, apply whether in business (he has a couple of small businesses) or in sport. He took over the captaincy of the side after four disappointing seasons. 'I felt the players we had at the club were far better than the performances we achieved,' he said. 'Having been there for many years, I didn't want to see the club deteriorating.' Smith says he has 'surprised himself' by enjoying the responsibility and thinks it has done him the world of good, both in management of people and decision making. 'I have surprised myself, and fortunately the success in Hampshire over the past year has been far greater than in the four previous years.'

> I do believe there are a lot of parallels between being a successful sportsman and being a successful businessman. The most important thing I feel that has worked this year is just communication throughout the squad, to make them feel special and to make them feel good about themselves. There has been such a huge transformation. The side itself hasn't changed very much but our performances have been so much better – I think because everyone feels so much part of the team. We are working as one and pulling in the same direction. Anyone here who is involved in management and managing people will agree.

Taking the trouble to try to understand the individuals in a team is vital. Smith says that he is 'if anything, probably a little soft, not a huge disciplinarian' – to behave otherwise, he believes, would be excessive.

> I believe that when you get to that stage, you know your own body and what you can and can't do. At the end of the day, you're not letting yourself down, but the rest of the team down. If we go down we go down together. Encouragement is so important. If somebody does something wrong you have to let them know, or reprimand them, and make sure they do ultimately know who the boss is. There are people who take a lot more than they should. As long as you can differentiate between those and the others – everybody needs to be treated differently. You have to try to understand individuals and what makes them tick. Some need reprimands; some need you to be more relaxed. Some need confidence and others not as much. As a captain, if you can try to understand people, you're half way there.

The recurring theme that emerges from all those whose success is intertwined with the efforts of other people is this: people must be allowed responsibility for some part of the campaign. They must feel that they have contributed and that their contribution is noticed and valued.

Michael Lynagh, who captained Australia in 1987 and then for three years from 1992, until he retired, discovered that delegation was effective in areas where he felt others knew more than he did. He also had to make an effort to become more outgoing, but again, adapted the management of the team to his own disposition and worked more on a one-to-one basis than in the inspirational style that had worked for his more flamboyant predecessor, Nick Farr-Jones.

As a captain I got guys within the team who had experience and I delegated, basically. I could look after the backs – because I had done that for many years with Nick – but with the forwards, I got key people within the forwards to look after them, to stir them up and do what forwards do. I also realized I had to change a little bit to become a better captain. I became more assertive in terms of team meetings, where I had been quite happy to listen and work things out later. Now I had to lead the meetings, and that was quite a change of direction for me.

That was good for me in terms of personal development but it was something that I had to do as a captain. When you're dealing with guys who are fairly élite sportsmen you don't really need to motivate them. Before a game, it's more pointing the herd in the right direction and keeping them together. I was very heavily involved in planning. Motivation wasn't really an issue, but bringing all that individual motivation to gel together was more my role.

I used to do that in a different way to Nick, who was quite an orator, and would stand up and away he'd go. He'd talk for hours and he'd be terrific. I'd go and spend time with individual people within the team. I'd make the effort, maybe, to go and have breakfast with somebody, and then have lunch with somebody else, and a cup of coffee in the afternoon with somebody else, and that took me out of my comfort zone.

[Before my captaincy] I used to have guys I was comfortable with and would spend a lot of time with. [After being appointed captain] instead of playing golf in the afternoon with my regular mates, I'd make an effort to go and talk to other people, which was great fun. I'd see how they were going, how they were feeling, if they were happy. That was important to me because if they're not happy, their motivation wanes. It was more on a one-to-one basis. The guys could see that I was doing this, they could see I was trying, and they reacted accordingly, so there was good feedback for me.

Lynagh found he enjoyed the responsibility of management despite feeling that he did not have a natural inclination towards it.

My one problem was that I'm a fairly quiet and reserved person. As captain you do have to make an effort to be heard and have points of view and talk to people. Nick Farr-Jones was very good at that. He was a very outgoing and personable person and that's why we made such a good team, I thought, when he was captain and I was vice-captain. I looked after everything behind him and he looked after everything in front of him on the pitch. Off the pitch we were very good friends but had very different personalities. In a way we complimented one another very well. When Nick retired and I took over, I had to reinvent myself a little bit. I tried that – but also, if I stood in the dressing room and started thumping the table and swearing at the forwards and saying, 'Come on, you've got to do this and that', they wouldn't have taken me seriously, because they know it's not me. Part of captaincy is delegating to people who are in a position to do that, and that's what I did. I got people within the team who were experienced and I got them as my deputies. They weren't necessarily vice-captains or leaders, but they were leaders of mine within that team and within groups of that team. That's how I overcame my shyness in terms of being a captain.

Lynagh found that discipline came from within the team, without the manager or coach stepping in.

One of the guys would quietly have a word and say what wasn't acceptable to the Australian Wallaby team, and what was. All those things had evolved over a period of time. Success helps with all this, but part of success is being a good squad; being not only a good rugby team but a good group of people that other people want to be around and be involved with, and that's what we were at that time.

The first time I ever had somebody tell me that the curfew was midnight was when I came to Saracens and went on a pre-season trip up to Newcastle. I played for under-16 teams and under-18 teams, the schoolboy teams, but this was the first time I had ever been given a curfew. When we came back at 10 minutes to midnight there were the coaches sitting there in the foyer ticking you off. I thought, 'this is not right, discipline has got to come from within the group, otherwise it's them and us and it's not a team.' It was an interesting comparison with what I had been used to.

At Chelsea Football Club, the management style of Ken Bates has been compared to a fiefdom or dictatorship. Bates believes, however, that there are other fiefdoms in existence apart from his own.

I think a benevolent dictatorship is a good way of running a country. At least Mussolini got the trains to run on time, but he wasn't benevolent. By and large, what we try to do is to get good people and give them their own fiefdom and let them run it to get results. Perhaps it's a bit like Sam Chisholm, who's just retired from Sky. His style was to delegate everything and then interfere like hell – not a bad philosophy.

The right recruits for Chelsea, Bates says, are 'youngish, hungry, want to prove themselves and be given an environment in which they are allowed to flourish and make their own decisions.'

Chay Blyth's early experiences of management were as a sergeant in the Parachute Regiment. He enjoyed wielding power and declined a commission: 'An officer is there for strategy, sergeants are there for discipline and for holding the thing together. Therefore you're really quite a powerful person and I thought I'd lose that power.' Blyth showed an instinctive feel for another management strength: being on the side of those he managed. On his own admission, this could have landed him in jail when a young lieutenant from Sandhurst, dispatched to Bahrain, where Blyth was a platoon commander, decided that a foot inspection should follow a 10-mile run. Blyth had other views, but the officer insisted. When the officer came to do the inspection, however, the barracks was empty because Blyth had 'told them to bugger off'.

Even in extreme conditions at sea, Blyth says, the same tenets apply: give people responsibility and let them run with that responsibility.

> It's quite difficult, particularly on a boat if you're racing. It can be a guy's job to trim the sail and you can think, 'Jesus, it's not quite right, I want to do it myself.' But you have to let them get on with it. The same applies to business, of course. Given responsibility, they will rise to that occasion. Unfortunately, we live in an umbrella society; we're all protecting our backsides and our backs and we tend to be a bit careful of letting go of stuff, because of the possibility of flak coming in our direction.

Like Horlick, he stresses that people have to be carefully chosen for this strategy to work. He describes his managers as 'hand picked. They run their particular department, whatever it is. It's terrific, I don't have to worry about it. One manager has just signed a contract for 10 boats the other day, and I haven't even seen the contract. It'll be all right; I know it'll be all right.'

Blyth says that people management on a yacht is the same as it is business. He learnt a never-forgotten lesson: a manager has to have feedback, has to learn from it, and has to do more than criticize.

> I started off in the Parachute Regiment, as an NCO dealing with a small team, as a corporal with a bigger team, then a sergeant with a bigger team. With my crew on *Great Britain 2*, although we won nine out of 12 trophies, when we had the review process, the thing that came through was that I was quick to criticize and slow to praise. It absolutely stung me to death, and I've tried to avoid it ever since. At the end of the day, as we all know, it's people.

For the super chef, the temptation has always been to mould students in the image of the master. It takes a passionate individual, says Raymond Blanc, to become a brilliant chef. If he or she is also to manage a kitchen that does not deteriorate into a blood bath, there has to be some management thinking.

> At last today our industry is regaining its credibility and respectability and so much has changed in so little time. Today, a chef must not only be a craftsman but also a manager. His responsibilities are daunting. He controls, teaches, guides and encourages a complete brigade from 10–70 people. He has both complete creative and commercial responsibilities. He is also for health and safety and too many other tasks to mention. That is an awesome task for anyone. On top of that you add the tremendous pressure of the heat in your face, the proximity, the speed and the expectation of every guest. A modern chef has not been taught to cope with all these factors, he has not been taught to be a manager. Although I do not condone it, sometimes tempers do flair in the kitchen. It is now such a commercially competitive arena that we need to teach our chefs commercial and management skills to prepare for the challenge ahead. At Le Manoir, we certainly have taken that challenge.

Forty per cent of the Michelin-starred chefs working in Britain have gone through Blanc's kitchen: Gary Jones, Marco Pierre White, Paul Heathcote, Brunot Loubet, Michael Caine, Richard Neat. For Blanc, part of the challenge has been to stand back and allow their own creativity and individuality to come through. Ideals and principles should be instilled, but excessive control discouraged.

> Every Blanc student has his own expression. I am trying to be so careful not to damage those people or damage their own creativity, their own presence, their own expression. I have not marked them to the point where they are created, where they can say they are a Blanc object. They are not. Mostly what they have in common is that passion, that enthusiasm. I am very proud of it. Teaching, I think, is one of the most wonderful things that can happen to you in that position. To have these youngsters come in fresh from college or elsewhere and just crafting them, making them grow bigger, so that eventually the ideals I have will belong to them and will serve them all their life.

Blanc runs a team of chefs at Le Manoir aux Quat'Saisons and, more recently, has established Petit Blancs, serving simpler food, in

Oxford, Cheltenham, Birmingham and Manchester (autumn 2000). For these to succeed, he has had to recruit carefully. 'One part of success is surrounding yourself with the best people who have earned your trust. I think I have that in each of the units I own. Each of the managers and chefs are the very best. They are self-motivated, have everything in place, and I don't feel the quality will go down.'

Roger Black learned about poor management in 1991 when he was one of the runners in the 4 × 400-metres relay. The runners discussed how to outflank the favourites, the Americans, and concluded that they would depart from the perceived wisdom about the running order. Black, the fastest, would run first instead of last. Black recalls: 'One of the team managers said something that I think is an example of good management: if you really believe in each other as a team, you must do this.' The other said, as he walked out of the room, 'Be it on your heads.' The team changed the running order, got a head start, and won. Effective management, Black believes, is above all about being capable of listening to a sincere contribution from capable team members, and there is no glow like that of shared achievement.

> That to me was such a wonderful moment. Individual success is great, but you can't share it with anybody really. What I have done as an individual is mine, and I can remember those moments, and it's great. When you achieve as part of winning team, you have it for the rest of your life. We have that bond for the rest of our lives. That's why I liked teamwork when I was at school. To me, ultimate success comes through teamwork.

Managing an office or a business is one thing: managing a (sometimes temperamental) celebrity quite another. So says Harvey Goldsmith, who has tried it – with Billy Connolly and Van Morrison, among others – and backed away. He realized that he preferred the less intense relationships he enjoyed as a promoter.

> Management is quite difficult, it's like marriage – you have to be able to respect each other and the roles you play, while also having a real relationship with the person you're working with, and it's often difficult

and terribly intense. And it's 24 hours a day; you're a psychiatrist, a wet-nappy service, mentor, businessman, accountant – you do everything but sing and dance and play the guitars, and sometimes you have to do that! So it's very difficult, but for me it's very different, as I enjoy the variety of flicking from one artist to the next. I get a buzz much stronger moving out of one circumstance to another, as opposed to having an intense relationship with one particular person, which can be very difficult and debilitating. It has its highs and lows but, to me, it's like having a second marriage.

Chay Blyth's transformation from intrepid yachtsman to successful businessman, who translated his own knowledge about challenge into a buoyant concern, brought with it particular insights into leading others. His skippers have to do this under testing conditions. Does the leader also have to be seen to do everything better than the led? Blyth says not:

> If you'd asked me three years ago, I'd have said 'yes'. Particularly in yachting, that's not the case now. This came to light in the last BT Global Challenge, when Humphrey Walters, chief executive of a management training organization called Mast, went on the race himself. His idea was to study the management relationship between the skippers and their crews, and he wrote a book about it. One of the things that came out was that the leader definitely doesn't have to know everything about everything. I tell our people that now. They should see what resources they've got and suck that information from that resource, and get them to help you all the time. What they have to be able to do is decide, having got that information, what is important and what isn't.

Another seminal truth about managing other people successfully comes from Ken Bates: 'People who don't make mistakes don't make anything. The one thing I object to is someone making the same mistake twice. There are lots of other mistakes and you don't want to do the same one twice, do you?'

Another is that it is a mistake to expect managing people to be an easy ride. Sometimes, inevitably, they don't like what they hear. Smith says that this has to be accepted, and the manner of delivery honest.

When I tell players they won't be playing I expect them to be unhappy and to ask all sorts of questions. I wouldn't expect anything different. I'd be disappointed if they didn't kick up some sort of fuss, because it's their livelihood I'm playing with. Today was a difficult day; we had to make one or two changes in our side. To drop someone is really difficult. I was nearly in tears when I told this friend of mine he wouldn't be playing on Sunday. You need to be honest and approach whoever you are talking to and speak from your heart. You cannot lie about why he's not playing. I think they respect my honesty and they have responded by going back to the second team in good spirit. They have continued to work hard at their game and they've been brilliant.

Managing other people can enhance your own performance, Smith believes:

When you watch a game of cricket, in my experience, it looks a lot harder when you're sitting and watching than it actually is out in the middle. Sometimes, if you have fast bowlers you think, 'God, how am I going to score a run when I get out in the middle?' Taking over as captain has helped a lot because I can't show too many nerves or a lot of the younger players in the side will think I don't seem to have things under control.

6 Lady luck – being in the right place at the right time

I was 35 at the time, young enough for pop stars not to think me a boring old fart, old enough to talk to Dame Edith Evans and not be treated like a child. It was a perfect age.

Michael Parkinson, TV interviewer

There are two schools of thought on luck and the more down-to-earth says that you make your own. As feature writer Vicki Woods wrote when she profiled Michael Parkinson in 1998, on his return to the *Parkinson* show: 'Parkinson always followed his luck (and you have to be clever to be lucky, as any Fleet Street editor will smugly tell you).'

Brilliant careers are not founded on luck, but good luck – fate, karma, kismet, providence, call it what you will – always appears somewhere. Being born to the right people can be a tremendous contributor towards a successful life, as anyone would surely acknowledge. For those without the congenital silver spoon, being in the right place at the right time can be exactly what it takes.

David Lloyd, who played tennis for Britain and then founded the David Lloyd fitness centres, had it about right when he said (in a Robert Half Interview, as it happens): 'You need a lot of luck. I don't care what you do, but you need luck along the way. You make a lot of your own, but you still have to have it – it's got to break for you.'

At this point, we should zoom in on Michael Parkinson, born luckily into a supportive family in a warm mining community. Parkinson was indeed fortunate. He was born in the right place, with the right accent, when British society was undergoing a seismic change. Parkinson had useful talents and attributes to begin with (see chapter 1) – and, importantly, he also had the right interests, in sport, theatre and film – but he also had the luck not merely of the draw, but of the epoch. It was a good time to be born clever and northern.

> I was in the right place at the right time. Before the 1960s I couldn't have got a job as a doorman at the BBC because of my accent. It wasn't allowed. I was a producer at Granada, my first job in television, when the 1960s revolution happened. It was fascinating. Nobody had actually quite pinned down what happened, but it opened floodgates. It allowed people like me, with an accent such as I have, to become not just accepted, but to become searched out, wanted, fashionable. We were given this wonderful boost to our careers by the fact that we spoke the way we did. That was probably as crucial as anything in my career, just that wonderful moment of timing.

Parkinson probably has The Beatles to thank as much as anyone for the northern fervour that carried him along.

> When I was with Granada, I was producing this show called *Scene at Six Thirty*. The Beatles were our resident group! We had them on the show, these kids, who talked like that, whom nobody knew. One day they went away to London and they came back and there were 20,000 kids running down Cross Street after them. All this started happening then – the north-country writing, the actors. It was a wonderful liberating time, and it changed our world.

Parkinson's brilliant timing coincided with other useful social phenomena: the grammar schools opening up new worlds to clever working-class children; the lack of pressure to achieve; the fostering of sport. It was not a classless society but, as Vicki Woods points out in her witty and perceptive profile in *The Observer*, a Michael Parkinson born today in the same social circumstances would not find it so easy:

He was lucky, there's no denying. You couldn't do it now, could you? In Blair's Britain? You couldn't take some underclass kid from a Cudworth council estate and shove him blazered and tied into a decent school with no fees payable, could you? You couldn't then watch him diddle around aimlessly, dreaming of playing cricket for Yorkshire, get two miserable exam passes in English and religious studies and hurl him none the less into the finishing school of an officers' mess, could you? With a load of patronizing young Sloanes to set himself against and vow to o'erleap? Could you buggery (to employ a Parkinsonism).

Parkinson's wonderful timing also encompassed the burgeoning TV stations. When the _Parkinson_ show came along, he was lucky again – lucky enough to be 35 and old enough to deal not only with fame, but with some of his guests. Vicki Woods again:

Once demobbed, Parkinson went to Fleet Street, where he became a professional northerner (it was fashionable then), and from Fleet Street to Sydney Bernstein's bright new Granada TV. He hit commercial television when all that world was young, lad, and all the trees were green, and Granadaland was a place where all the trees grew money. He was hard working, he was tough, he was ambitious and he was lucky. He followed his luck and changed jobs often... and then lucky, lucky Parky became fabulously famous with _Parkinson_, at the level-headed age of 35, which is still young enough to have a golden future and to hold on to what you've got instead of poking it all up your nose.

The epoch offered up yet more gems to Michael Parkinson: these were the days before public relations gurus and pre-planned, pre-approved, tame celebrity interviews. The world of Hollywood was ripe for the plucking. The great stars were available; and they were not accompanied by a minder from the film company vetoing the questions and ensuring a plug for some film. Not that these people were necessarily easy, as Parkinson points out:

I was 35 at the time, young enough for pop stars not to think me a boring old fart, old enough to talk to Dame Edith Evans and not be treated like a child. It was a perfect age... Also, it was timely – the right time to do a talk show. It was the end of the wonderful Hollywood star system, so I had the pick of those great names, which literally aren't there any more now. There were Bette Davis and Fred Astaire – he had never been inside a television studio to an interview before – and James Cagney, who had never done a TV interview in his life.

Parkinson's big breakthrough was an interview with Orson Welles. It was his first season, and the offer was for eight shows as a fill-in. But his producer – luck again – believed there was greater potential for the *Parkinson* show. There was simply nothing like it on TV at the time. 'We're going to get one guest who will actually turn everybody's head and make the agent think this is not just a fill-in.' It was not straightforward. Welles agreed to appear on condition that he could lie down on the plane over from France, where he was filming. British Airways agreed to take out two seats and a mattress was put in. Welles walked in and sat in a seat.

Once at the BBC, the deputy director-general's chair had to be fetched for him because he was so huge. Then he destroyed Parkinson's meticulously researched questions. Dressed entirely in black – 'about 9 foot tall' – he asked to see the questions then tore them up. It is a testament to Parkinson's skills, and nothing to do with luck, that they did two one-hour shows, and, Parkinson says, could have done 10. The dialogue flowed. It was a huge success. Parkinson says: 'That was the breakthrough. From that point on, every agent we went to thought, well, if Orson Welles will do this show, why wouldn't others? It was the perfect choice.'

The era in which Parkinson was carving out his career seems, by comparison with today, blissfully uncomplicated, as it did for Chay Blyth. Bright and capable, he was rapidly promoted to the rank of sergeant in the Army at the age of 21 because his boss at the time was keen to move away from 'dead men's shoes'.

That's timing, but it's also something that managers don't do – they don't look, or a lot of them don't. The Army's got a wonderful system of starting to look for leaders early on and bringing them on, up the ranks. They picked me up from there. When I became a sergeant, it wasn't so much just my ability – it happened to coincide with a boss who wanted to change the whole system from dead men's shoes. He promoted younger people and I happened to be the youngest of that particular group. Again, it was timing.

There was also an element of luck in the way Blyth launched the highly successful challenge business through which amateur sailors take part in a round-the-world race. He had negotiated with British Steel to have the boat (no luck there, just skilful negotiation), and with the French equivalent of the ocean racing club to find out whether it would be acceptable for his crew to pay for their passage (no luck there, just organization). Then a journalist came down to write about the chartering idea.

> I told him about this idea and he asked how much it was going to be. I had costed it, and in that split second I thought I had nothing to lose, so I doubled the cost. He ran a story in the _Daily Mirror_, and I filled the boat up from that one article. So we knew there were people out there who wanted challenge – after all, how else can you get on a boat to race round the world? How many people have got the skills to get on an ocean racer to race around the world – how can they get on a Whitbread boat or a Vendée boat? I thought that if we could build a fleet of boats, and keep the cost down by making them exactly the same, perhaps we could do a little business. Sure enough, it seems to work.

Harvey Goldsmith believes his life has been blessed. 'Basically I've had a slightly charmed life, a fantastic opportunity. I've seen the world in style; been to the most bizarre places, seen extraordinary things, played with artists, performers and stars most people couldn't get near. I was extremely lucky and I've enjoyed every minute of it.'

We return to this, however: luck always has to be helped. Goldsmith could have turned down the jaunt that resulted in his meeting Billy Connolly. He was putting on The Who in Glasgow. The show had just begun when the manager of the theatre, Greens Playhouse, dragged him away to the Kings Theatre.

He dragged me down to the theatre 20 minutes after The Who went on. I could hear this laughter coming from outside. Here was this strange, bearded person with the biggest pair of banana-shaped feet I had ever seen in my entire life. The audience were just clutching their sides with laughter, hanging off the boxes in the balconies. I couldn't understand a single word he was saying, not a word. Just looking at this guy I started to laugh. I had no idea why I was laughing.

Billy Connolly, through a great stroke of luck, was a great fan of The Who. Goldsmith was taken backstage to meet him, and Connolly said he would give anything to meet The Who. So began Goldsmith's relationship with Connolly and later, with Connolly's wife-to-be, Pamela Stephenson, both of whom he managed.

By coincidence, Michael Parkinson was also in Glasgow at the same time, making a personal appearance, and by even more remarkable coincidence he was forced to listen to Billy Connolly by a persistent taxi driver whose cab he got into to go to the airport.

The driver said to me 'Have you heard of the Big Yin?' and I said 'The big what?' He drove me past Greens Playhouse in Glasgow, which was starring the Big Yin, and said 'That's your man', and I said 'So what, to the airport please.' The driver stopped outside a parade of shops, as I grew irritated in the back, and came out with a tape of Billy Connolly Live. I took it home and two weeks later, my eldest boy, Andrew, told me to play it. I did, and booked Connolly the next day. He came on the show and did the joke about parking the bike up the person's backside, and from that point on…I mean, I didn't discover Billy Connolly, I just accommodated him. I was lucky. To unearth somebody like Connolly was one of the great perks of the job, because I've no doubt he's the funniest man on the planet. He's made me laugh more than anybody else.

Nicola Horlick says luck has helped her to rise up the career ladder very fast, although some strategic decisions of her own have helped.

I regret what happened with Morgan Grenfell, but I'm not sure that was really within my control. I was very sad when I left Mercury, because leaving Leonard [Licht] was very very hard. I was always going to live in his shadow, and I had to stand on my own two feet, but it was hard. I cried non-stop for about two weeks. It was like a divorce. I don't think I have too many regrets. On the whole, I've had a lot of luck and I've been surrounded by some exceptionally wonderful people both above and below me, who have supported me. I hope I have behaved well towards them and expressed my gratitude when they've helped me out, which they have.

Few people could regard a flunked A level – thus falling short of the grades needed for a university place – as lucky. Roger Black does, although at the time, knowing he had messed up his maths paper, it seemed like the worst day of his life. The grade D he achieved meant he had to put off his medical studies for a year. In the end, he went to university a year later, but left after a term to pursue a career in athletics.

I ran at school but didn't enjoy it; I liked team sports. I wanted to be a doctor and had to get a grade B in maths to go university, but one question flummoxed me. I kept trying to get the answer and couldn't and panicked – so much that I only completed half the paper. I remember leaving that exam room knowing I wasn't going to get the grade I needed, and it was the worst day of my life. It was also the best day of my life because a few weeks later I got the results. I got a D and got rejected from university. It meant I had a year off.

I took the exam again and got a grade B and got a place, but a friend said to me I was very talented, but talent wasn't enough, and that I should go and train with Kriss Akabusi and Todd Bennett at Southampton Athletics Club. That's what I did. Two months later I was running indoors for Great Britain. The truth is, if I had got a grade B that afternoon, I wouldn't be here and you wouldn't have a clue who I was. I would never have run, and I always remember that because it taught me that you don't really know what is going to happen to you. You go with the flow.

I ran, but I still went to university because I still wanted to be a doctor. At the end of the first term, I realized I had to make a decision between becoming a doctor and becoming an athlete. It was the biggest decision of my life, which was going to shape my life, but it was made easier by one of my professors. He said, 'Black, there are two ways to get a degree from Southampton University. You can spend the next five years here studying medicine, cut up dead bodies, do microbiology. At the end of those five years you will be totally stressed out – as all doctors are – but you will become a doctor. The other way is to leave now and become a full-time athlete. Train for three hours a day, spend three months every year in California, go to the Olympic Games, get paid to run, get paid to wear running shoes, become famous, but more importantly, lad, you can have 10,000 women screaming at you.' Obviously, I chose athletics. Five years later I got an honorary degree from the university.

There is an interesting facet to Roger Black's luck: it is connected with his overall view of life, that his cup is never half empty, but always half full.

7 Personal disasters and how they can help

Then there was an almighty crack and the window split. The water came up like Niagara Falls upside down. It went straight up in the air for a second or two. Then it settled down and it just kept coming. I'm slowly freezing, my body temperature is dropping all the time, now the window's broken, now the boat is full of water. This gave me the opportunity to swim out through the hole.

Tony Bullimore, trans-Atlantic sailor, on the moment the second 'impossibility' struck his already capsized racing yacht 1,500 miles from land

All careers have disasters and most brilliant careers have big disasters. Honestly. The higher the achievement, the further there is to fall. The distinguishing feature of the successful is that they dust themselves down (providing they survive, which most of them do) and get failure into some sort of perspective. They put it into its box, if you like, and move on. The most resourceful may even gain from it. It is certainly the case that, as Ken Bates said earlier, people who don't make mistakes don't make anything (although he goes on to add, 'The one thing I object to is someone making the same mistake twice').

Tony Bullimore's disaster at sea, graphically described above, and which we will come to later, is at one extreme of the scale. Most of us risk somewhat less than our necks, although when the sickening stench of failure is all around, and dreams are shattered and ambitions destroyed, it may not seem so. For an optimistic slant on failures, who better to go to than the spectacularly ill-fated Baldrick – or, at least, his alter-ego Tony Robinson:

> You mess up don't you? You make decisions and you mess up. The great thing about messing up, it seems to me, is that you only learn from your mess-ups. I have never learnt from my successes because what can you learn? I got it right! Big deal! You forget success so easily because feeling nice doesn't last long, feeling really terrible leaves an impression forever. All those mistakes, all those real mess-ups, they are still in here. They are presents to you really.

Shame is a major component of failure, especially in times when adventures in both business and sport are conducted under close media scrutiny. When Sebastian Coe ran a poor 800-metres race at the Moscow Olympics in 1980 – coming second when he was two seconds faster than anyone else in the race – the media descended like furies. Coe says: 'In the 800 metres in Moscow I learnt how not to behave 20 minutes before an Olympic final and in the 1500 metres I think I learnt the right way to do it.' The *News of the World* did not wait for the result of the 1500 metres (in which Coe won the gold medal), displaying a photograph of him on a training run the day afterwards with the caption: 'Coe's trail of shame'.

Public humiliation is a crushing force, but there are two useful facts to bear in mind. The first is that newspapers are wrapping chips within 48 hours (or they were, before newsprint was ruled too unhygienic for wrapping food, even chips) and the second was voiced by Ron Dennis, managing director of the TAG McLaren racing team some three years ago. 'The most important thing is not what people think of you, but what you think of yourself,' he said.

The significance of this remark is that when Dennis said it, his team was having its least successful period ever, apparently unable to win a major championship despite its history of fabulous triumphs. Shortly after he said it – at a Robert Half Interview – the fortunes of McLaren (now linked with Mercedes) turned again. A different character could have given up; the brilliant never do.

Our subjects have all been visited by disaster in varying concentrations. In this chapter we will pore over the smoking coals of misfortune and bad judgement; firstly because it makes the rest of us feel better to hear that the brilliant are not blessed with unbroken good fortune; and secondly because we all need to fail and to understand how we can turn setbacks to our advantage.

Two of our subjects fall into a special category: misfortune catapulted them into celebrity. Tony Bullimore's yacht – his unbreakable, indestructible yacht – broke up in the Southern Ocean (in nautical terms, the middle of nowhere). Nicola Horlick, pursuing a successful career in the City, suddenly found herself all over the newspapers when she was suspended from her job.

Bullimore was two months into the Vendée Globe race (which the best yachtsmen finish in 120 days, but which most do not finish at all), when the keel of his boat snapped. It was not a design fault – the structural engineer, from British Aerospace, had worked on his boats over the past 20 years and was 'first class'. Bullimore believes that the boat went past its safe working load.

> The keel shouldn't snap. It's like the back axle on a car; it's not supposed to break off. My yacht was made of carbon, with a foam-sandwich hull. The keel board was actually made of hollow carbon, which went down 17 feet. At the bottom of this it had four-and-a-half tons of lead bolted on to it. Inside the carbon, which is an aerodynamic shape, it's got a very big plate of stainless steel, which would never come out. I was in enormous, mountainous seas, and I think I got knocked down on a big beam sea. I've got knocked down; the keel board has swung up. As it's come up, a big wave has hit it and it's shuddered right up; to the hard spot, which is immediately under the hull and – bang! – it's snapped off. I heard it go crack! It was really quite amazing.

Yachtsmen capsize all the time, but Bullimore was in one of the least accessible places in the world.

> I was in one of the most desolate spots you could possibly be in at sea. There's a famous triangle in the Southern Ocean, Cape Town as one

point and Perth as another... The amazing thing was that before I got into that incredible storm – which meteorologists call a Bomb – I actually looked at my chart. I had a mug of tea, and I was dunking in my McVities biscuits, and I thought, 'It's quite amazing; I'm right on the corner of that magic triangle.' I had to go east and north and was coming up to about 50 degrees south, getting nearer to where you've got a chance if anything goes wrong. It was only a day away, then the big storm slowly, slowly came. I was sitting there looking up at the wind instruments. The wind was just fluttering on 80 knots. I had a safety harness all ready, hooked on. Before I could go on deck I had to hook on to a pad eye just outside the companionway entrance, because it was too dangerous to go on deck; you'd get chucked all over the place, and the sea was washing over the boat.

I was popping up on deck checking that I still had two masts and everything was there, going back down, sitting there, looking at the wind conditions. Every now and then I'm getting knocked down. When people write books about the sea – especially people like Alex Rose, Francis Chichester, Chay Blyth – they talk about getting knocked down twice when they go round the world. I was getting knocked down literally every half an hour. I'd just fall off another wave. Monohulls, even if you turn turtle – rolling right over – should come up the right way. Then there was an almighty crack and it took a second for my yacht to capsize.

How I didn't get hurt I don't know. I rolled over with the boat, and I was standing there saying 'come up, up you come, up you come' for a few seconds. There was no water in the boat, everything was shut up tight. Then I said to myself, 'The keel.' You get this horrible feeling, you always imagine you are going to lose the keel when you go down there. I was 800 miles from the Antarctic and 1500 miles from Perth.

Bullimore found himself instantly in survival mode. As he looked round the keel, perfectly upside down, he thought first of getting out alive and secondly of fire damage. The sea was churning around him – surreally, he noticed its greenish colour through the large windows – and he reached for his roll-up tobacco and papers, provided by one of his shore crew (although he had given up smoking). He stood smoking, working out how he was going to turn over his tiny two-ring burner, gas bottle and batteries. He thought he would have to lose the engine.

I was just working it out. That's all there was to it. At the time I said to myself, 'I can't step off, I can't. The only way I'm going to be saved is for someone to come to me.' I began to wonder who was going to come all the way down there. I was in international waters. Although we all claim to own the oceans, no one wants to be responsible outside their own territorial waters. I was gradually getting the feeling that I was in a sticky position this time. I sat there for something like four of five hours, looking at the chart and trying to work out how I could turn the inside of my capsized boat into a habitable cocoon for me to stay in, maybe for weeks.

I didn't have much food in there but I had a lot of food under the cockpit sole, which was all sealed, hatches closed. I couldn't get to there from inside the boat. It meant I had to open the companionway entrance, which would mean I would have to let the water in, which wasn't good news, because I would have to let it fill up before I could get out and then swim for food. Eventually I knew I would have to open a port light and get my distress beacon to go up to the surface, which was probably about seven feet. It would have to be tied up good and proper because if I let the distress beacon give out a mayday signal, and it floated away from the boat, I would be in dead trouble then. I thought, 'Survival is the name of the game.' It was as simple as that.

Then things got worse. A boom from one of the masts was tapping on one of the big windows, which was made of 12 ml high-tensile perspex, a tough plastic capable of withstanding hammer blows. Bullimore was confident that the material would stand up it. Then there was an almighty crack and the window split.

The water came up like Niagara Falls upside down. It went straight up in the air for a second or two. Then it settled down and it just kept coming. I'm slowly freezing, my body temperature is dropping all the time, now the window's broken, now the boat is full of water. This gave me the opportunity to swim out through the hole. I swam part way out with the beacon made fast to the inside of the boat and popped it up to the surface with the mayday light switched on. Then it's up there ticking away. That's got to send a signal to a satellite, satellite to an earth station, an earth station to the rescue services and then the rescue services have to send messages to maritime rescue services in Canberra. They then send out messages to the Royal Australian Navy, which have to decide what to do. I wasn't sure whether it was working because you have no means of knowing. You switch it on, there's a little light that flashes on and off very slowly, and you have got to believe that it's working.

The boat was filling with water, and the airspace was being used up. Bullimore made a mark on the side of the boat and four or five hours later, the sea was an inch higher. The lack of air made it inevitable that he would have to leave the hull eventually. Meanwhile he waded and swam around inside, freezing cold, before deciding to risk swimming out to try to free the life raft with a knife. The fascinating aspect of this horror tale is Bullimore's reaction.

It's a funny thing, but I have had problems before and I know what I'm doing. I'm pretty good at survival and have had survival training. It is a known quantity situation with me. The deeper I get into the mire, to put it bluntly, the calmer I become. When I'm on my own I can look at the situation. I spend a lot of time thinking about it, and it might be done in two minutes, but it will be done. It is incredibly important to keep the right frame of mind. You just don't get there if you're in a panic and feel that everything is just going to fall around you. You have got to go for it. It's the character of the person.

The Royal Australian Navy, unknown to Bullimore, was on its way. When their rescue boat arrived he was lying on a narrow shelf – it had been a low shelf, now it was a high shelf. He also had a bridle ready, so that he could tie himself up with his head above the water in case he fell asleep, or felt sick or dizzy.

I was lying there, and that might sound quite easy, but the boat is rolling badly and pitching, so the water inside the boat is churning round like a washing machine, and I'm getting it slapping in the face all the time. I'm trying to keep awake because I can keep my body temperature up more. All of a sudden I hear a noise. I thought it was a helicopter but it was an engine on a rib, a rigid hull inflatable, just ticking over.

Pictures had been beamed all over the world of Bullimore's upturned yacht. Everyone believed he was dead. When he struggled to the surface of the sea, swimming under the rigging, which could have caught him and caused him to drown so close to rescue, the emergency services were amazed. Physically, the extent of his injuries was hypothermia. Mentally, he was fine, turning down counselling and getting over the trauma with a couple of pints in a bar. The effect was on his attitude.

I think inwardly I have changed. I feel slightly different. I did make a big promise that I wouldn't be so gruff towards people. When I want things doing I tend to run at it and I think everyone else around me should be running – let's go for it, let's get it done. This is not only on the vessel but anywhere. Somehow, in my subconscious, I must have known I was a bit naughty towards people because that hit me like a bullet. Deep down I know I was a bit pushy. I have to watch it, because you need people, and it's nice to have people who want to help you, and it's nice to be nice to people – and there's a lot smarter people around than me.

My wife comes from Jamaica and all round Jamaica there were churches with a full house, people couldn't get into the church, and they were praying for me. I got letters from church people in Russia, Poland, Eastern Europe, Western Europe, America, Australia, New Zealand, South Africa, Africa, Hong Kong – and the strangest places – sending me good wishes and saying we all prayed so hard for you. I have friends who are Christian, Muslim, Jewish, and it was so lovely that it crossed the borders of different denominations and religions. I feel very warm that people prayed for me. I never thought other people would pray for me to be alive. It touches my heart.

Bullimore has a simple tenet for recovering from disaster: get back on the horse.

You know the old saying. It applies to everything. In my case, it was important because I don't know how long I've got left. It's important to me that I don't waste time. If I couldn't have got back on that boat and gone out sailing in Australia within a very short time, it would have worried me. If I'd said, 'No, I don't think I will' I wouldn't have had that 100 ft catamaran down in the docks.

Nicola Horlick, successfully ensconced with Deutsche Morgan Grenfell, had no inkling of the drama to come when she was summoned to the Lanesborough Hotel in London by a friend who held a senior position in ABN Amro. When she arrived, she recalls, a main board director 'leapt out from behind a pillar' and offered her a job running the bank's global asset management business. She declined because her eldest child was sick and the youngest just born. Only half the story got back to her employer, however, which promptly suspended her in the belief that she was about to decamp, taking her team with her. It was a Tuesday. Before she got home – and well before the following Friday, when she was due to return to the bank to discuss her position – news of her suspension emerged over the Reuters news wires. Horlick's husband and grandmother read it before she had a chance to tell them herself. Then the media descended on her doorstep.

It was a very strange experience. I felt I hadn't had my chance to say what actually happened, and that I ought to have had my chance. I tried to go on the Friday morning and say what I was going to say, but nobody would listen. So I said: 'OK, fine, I'll go to Frankfurt', and I did. I had a two-hour meeting with the head of personnel and legal services for the whole group. They listened and they were incredibly sympathetic, but by that stage it had all become so high profile that there wasn't really any chance I could be reinstated.

Bizarrely, Horlick had been promoted on the Friday before her suspension, which came in the middle of a new business presentation. 'The whole thing was just so bizarre and so extraordinary I just couldn't get my mind around it,' she says. It soon became clear that whatever the justice of the situation, she would not be given her job back. 'As the man in Frankfurt said, it had all become such a big issue that there wasn't really any going back. It was still unfair, but that was a bit irrelevant.'

The public, normally contented to view the City as an unfathomable enclave of rich-but-unknown operators, suddenly found a thirst for knowledge about Nicola Horlick. She was on the front page of all the national newspapers, red-painted mouth in a downward curve, eyes filled with tears, hair beautifully cut into a bob, trademark clothes black and expensive. Nicola Horlick shattered the image of successful professional women by crying in public – and not being ashamed of it – and re-shaped it in her own image. 'Having it all' became synonymous with her metropolitan lifestyle.

Behind this enviable persona, however, lay the catastrophe that made Nicola Horlick's upheaval at work seem trivial. Her first child, Georgina, was losing her 10-year battle against leukaemia. Horlick coped with it head on, researching the illness and challenging medical staff.

I was with Georgina the whole time she was very sick. She was an incredibly determined and very amazing person. Whenever she was out of hospital she absolutely insisted that she was going back to school. Not only was she going to go to school, but she was going to do every single after-school club or activity that she could possibly do. The only thing she couldn't do was swimming, because there are lots of bugs in swimming pools, and when you're immuno-suppressed, it is not a good place to go.

Since she was at school most days, she would leave at about 8.10 in the morning and come back at 5.20 and there didn't seem any need for me to be sitting at home. I would have been dwelling on the horror of the whole situation, so I just went to work. We slipped into this routine of just trying to be as normal as possible, which I think was good for her and very good for me, because it meant that she was very normal. I am absolutely convinced there is a major benefit both in terms of helping to fight the disease and in terms of just generally helping a family get through it, if the child who's sick is trying to live as normally as possible. Part of that was me going to work. I obviously wouldn't have done it if I thought it was damaging Georgie, or any of my children, in any way.

After Georgie's death, Horlick used her work as an avenue back to normality.

> When someone dies, whether it's your child, your mother or father, your husband or whatever, you really can't think straight. It sounds strange to say it was a shock when she'd had a bone marrow transplant and relapsed a couple of times, but we were actually beginning to feel that we were beginning to win. She had gone for six months post transplant without relapsing, and that was a very good sign. She was 100 per cent engrafted with the new marrow, so I think she would have survived if she hadn't been hit by an infection, which really came right out of the blue.
>
> It was a terrible shock. She got sick on the Sunday evening and could have died by the Tuesday if we had turned the machines off then. We decided we needed a bit more time, and that there could be a miracle. We got to Friday lunchtime and it was clear she was not going to survive. It was all very quick and sudden and we decided we would go away for a few weeks. We went away for three weeks to South Africa and it was surreal, because I went from being shut in a small room in Great Ormond Street for a year with Georgie to suddenly being in South Africa with the heat and the sunshine and the beautiful beaches. It was odd and surreal and in a way put the grief on hold. When we came back I came down to earth with a bump and I didn't really think. I thought I would stay at home until the end of January and see that the children were properly back at school and settled, then I would go to work and see how it went. That's what I did.

Horlick now finds that her every move is monitored by the press, who want to know every detail about her, from the colour of her sofa to her perfume. No part of her life is private. Her high profile has been used in advertising campaigns for her employer (although she made the advertising agency dilute the emphasis on her by including the rest of her team). She has been accused of courting the press but in fact, she says, cooperation is easier than letting speculation run riot: 'One thing I have learned is that if you completely ignore them, in some ways that's worse. You've somehow got to keep in touch, and keep talking. That's difficult, but I suppose it is just part of life now, and I just have to accept it.' Horlick adds: 'Yes, I do wish I was an anonymous person again.'

Those whose work is in the public eye also mess up in the public eye. Considering the hundreds of people Michael Parkinson has interviewed in public – many of them thoroughly cussed – his *faux pas* have been few. Forgetting John Wayne's name was one of them. 'I'd put "Duke" on top of my notes, and could only bring to mind Duke Ellington. It took me 15 minutes to remember his name. From that point on, I used to have the name plastered around the studio, whoever it was.'

Robert Mitchum, one of Parkinson's heroes, arrived stoned and monosyllabic, and answered every question 'yep' or 'nope'. Muhammad Ali called Parkinson 'a honky' and squared up to him because he believed Parkinson was going to ask him to read from a book (Ali was half-literate). Parkinson's father later said: 'Why didn't you thump him?' Then there was the encounter with Emu (managed by the late Rod Hull) in which Parkinson was wrestled to the floor, temporarily losing his cool but making great (and classic) television. Parkinson says that in his game of unnatural tete-à-tetes, asking the wrong question and occasionally saying or doing the wrong thing is human and inevitable.

> I'm sure I've asked questions I wished I hadn't many times. You phrase it wrongly, and you cringe when you see it back again. You think oh God, how inelegant that was, and how awful, but somehow you muddle through. It's a strange old job. The fascinating thing about it is that you can't rehearse it. It is this extraordinary accommodation between two people who are trying to pretend on air that they like each other, and probably don't.

There have been other gaffes. Parkinson is invariably asked for his opinion on other interviewers and, in 1999, in an interview with the *TV Times*, criticized the new breed of celebrity chat show hosts, including West Ham footballer Ian Wright, the Duchess of York and Melinda Messenger. Wright was offended and Parkinson promptly offered a fulsome apology: 'I responded in an over-vigorous manner on a subject I feel strongly about, but I did not mean it to be a personal attack on you. If it seemed that way and caused you hurt, then I apologise. I was trying to make a general point and made the mistake of seeming to personalise it.' Parkinson invited Wright and his manager to dinner. His rule of thumb: if you're wrong, admit it.

The one wrong leap in Parkinson's career was *TV-am*, of which he was a co-founder with David Frost, Angela Rippon, Robert Kee and Anna Ford, dubbed the Famous Five. The consortium won the franchise, but failed to run the station because (as Vicki Woods said in *The Observer* in her profile of Parkinson) they were 'comprehensively outmanoeuvred'. First the IBA delayed the launch until Channel 4 got started, then the BBC beat them in the breakfast television stakes by launching its own couple-on-a sofa from six till nine. Finally there were troubles with the board. Parkinson, thoroughly demoralized, began to drink and became depressed. It was his wife, Mary, who shooed him back into TV gently, with lightweight shows like *Give Us a Clue* and *Going for a Song*. The débâcle still ranked a decade later. Parkinson told Woods:

> We were shooed off the golden egg, basically. And all we had to do was sit on it and wait. We'd been given the licence to exclusively broadcast adverts between 6.30 and 9.30 am. How about that for a proposition? And if you couldn't get that right... what the hell. Big business... it's a mucky game.

Sebastian Coe's failures have been not just public but have generated huge public interest. Having retired from the rough and tumble of athletics, his next career – as MP for Falmouth and Camborne – was aborted by a general election. The Tories were routed, and Coe defeated. Did he shrug it off as an irrelevance? On the contrary. Losing the seat was, he says, as painful as missing a medal.

> Any MP who tells you that they enjoy standing in some windswept sports hall or village hall, or wherever it is on that wet Thursday night when 58,000 people hand you your P45 very publicly is, frankly, not

telling you the truth! I was very disappointed. I had committed myself mentally to seeing out my political career as the MP for Falmouth and Camborne but, as they say, the people spoke.

Coe is philosophical about failure. When he failed to win the 800 metres in Moscow, his father famously said that he 'ran like an idiot' and that he was 'humiliated and ashamed'. Coe was asked how that felt.

What he actually said – and he is a fairly brutal, honest bloke, and it was actually a very important part of the rehabilitation – was that we had not spent 10 years working two or three times a day from the age of 14 onwards on windswept Yorkshire moors and windswept, rainswept tracks, to run as badly as I did. It was an appalling race and I finished second. I actually found his observations perfectly acceptable. It was the hard men of Fleet Street who blanched about it.

What he was saying was a very honest observation, and it is the observation of a good manager. It wasn't a 'we win, you lose' syndrome. He was actually taking responsibility, and what he said was that he felt ashamed for himself, because he felt that he had a major contribution to this. We talked about it afterwards and in fairness, we both learnt they are the observations you don't make in front of the average tabloid journalist because you never have the time to explain the thinking and the ethos behind it.

What he was actually saying was, 'Don't just look at him, look at me. I am his coach, this is a guy who is a world record holder and on paper was two seconds faster than anybody else on the field and he goes out and on the biggest occasion runs like that! That is not just his problem, that is my problem because I have to take some responsibility in the way that I presented him on the line. I structured the training. Did I do enough mental preparation?

All those sort of things go through a good coach's mind, they don't walk away from it. That is a concept that, frankly, we could have spent the next 100 years trying to explain. They chose to write it up that way. It can sometimes be very helpful because if you ask me, one of the biggest motivations in bouncing back for the 1500 metres a few days later, was getting the Sunday newspapers in the village three days later. The front page of the *News of the World* displayed a photo of me on my training run the day after the 800 metres with 'Coe's trail of shame' written underneath.

Mary Peters, Coe's team manager, told him: 'You have run an appalling race, there's no point telling you that because you know it.' But he was lucky, she said. If he had been another athlete – for instance, Jim Ryan, the American world record holder, who was tripped over in 1972 by an unseeded African competitor – his Olympic career would have been over. But he could get back on to the track in four days' time and go out and win another title. Coe says: 'She was quite right. People who understand the history of their sport, or the history of whatever they are doing, find it very helpful when putting things into perspective.'

Perhaps predictably, Chay Blyth's disasters have all been at sea. The first, nearly 30 years ago, was on his round-the-world attempt. In the Southern Ocean, the same waters that broke up Tony Bullimore's yacht, a huge sea smashed his self-steering gear, and he was hurled across the cockpit, badly gashing his forehead. One night, he found himself on a collision course with a Russian fishing vessel. He threw an explosive charge in the air. There was a bang and a blinding flash, which brought the entire crew on deck.

More seriously, he and a colleague, Eric Blunn, were in the water for 19 hours during an attempt on the 109-year-old record from New York to San Francisco, set by the clipper-ship *Flying Cloud*. Their trimaran *Beefeater II* was overwhelmed in what Blyth calls 'the Everest of sailing. The waters at the tip of South America are routinely the worst in any ocean…We actually passed the Horn but were still in the shallows to the west of the Cape when the boat was overwhelmed. I hope I never see conditions like it again.'

The sea was crashing around them in v-shaped troughs, with crests towering over *Beefeater*. Their only aim – their only thought – was to get out of there as fast as possible.

It's all to do with project management. You have to decide what the objective is and you have to decide if you're going to go for it. We'd got 50–70 miles beyond Cape Horn and a gale got up and the waves went back very quickly. It was horrific, just horrific, and they don't let up, one comes up after the other, like legions marching at you one after the other. One was bigger than the other one and a multi-hull has no keel under it, so when you go over, it doesn't come up. You just have to have a sense of humour.

They were in the water for 19 hours.

You have to go into survival mode immediately. It became night-time very quickly, so at least we slept a little bit. But you're sort of sleeping in the water, quite difficult. The following day you've got to start doing things to keep yourself occupied in a meaningful way. I reckon we can last about five days before we pop off. The safest place to be is in the boat, so we cut a hole in the boat. Then one of us sat and watched for any ships or aircraft, in hope. You had to do something meaningful, and collate what was still left in the boat, so that you can still look at food and water. Eric is an ex-paratrooper as well, so we'd both seen death.

'Survive something like that and you begin to understand your own mortality,' Blyth says. The culture shock of the Southern Ocean, he says, is 'beyond imagination' – a fact he tried to impress upon the crews in the BT Global Challenge. For Blyth, the business of getting through a life-threatening disaster is tackled in the same way as a project in safer waters: assess the task, work out the moves, and carry them out. Most of all, stay focused on the objective.

If everyone has disasters, the secret of success must be how to handle them. One major technique – and one that many people never grasp – is refusing to allow mistakes or calamities to destroy your morale. The rule has to be this: make it, rectify it, learn from it, file it. No one else is wasting his or her day poring over your catastrophe; neither should you.

Sometimes, as this episode involving Harvey Goldsmith shows, you just have to let it ride, even when the central figure of your blooper is your hero (although you are certainly not his). Asked for his heroes, Goldsmith replies that Miles Davis, the legendary jazzman, is his ultimate, despite Goldsmith having had the salutary experience of being grabbed round the throat by him.

I was fortunate enough to tour Miles Davis, as difficult as he was, around Europe. The culmination was a show at the Rainbow at Finsbury Park, the best rock venue at the time. The equipment arrived in England four hours before the concert and we had to clear it through Customs. Then we laid on a large summer buffet for him, including a large tray of watermelon. Davis was already grumpy and played the whole concert with his back to the audience.

But when he came into the hospitality room and saw the buffet he exploded. He grabbed me by the throat, pinned me to the wall, and I won't tell you the expletive he used, but he asked whose idea it was to have the buffet. I said mine. He said I was taking the Michael. I couldn't work out what I had done. His hands were tightening round my throat and I thought he was going to kill me. The tour manager told me later that watermelons were the symbol of slavery.

Davis gave a brilliant second concert and soon afterwards, he and Goldsmith parted. 'I didn't say anything, he didn't say anything, we said our goodbyes.' About six months later he read that Davis had sent Diana Ross a T-shirt with a watermelon on it as she set off on a tour of Europe. He no longer considered watermelons an insult. 'So there you go. Miles Davis is a hero.'

Dealing with showbusiness egos requires exceptional sanguinity. Another of Goldsmith's heroes is Van Morrison, whom he managed. Van Morrison was living in Fairfax, California, when he sent over a postcard with a drawing of a house on it and the instruction to find it for him in London. Goldsmith, to his own amazement, found the very house not far from his own, in St Mary Abbott, and to his further amazement, it was available to rent. 'If this is how life works, I couldn't believe my luck.' Goldsmith recalls. 'I there and then signed up for the house and lease for a year and phoned Van Morrison up, as I was really excited. He caught the next flight over, went to the house, walked up the stairs, down the stairs, and asked to be taken back to the airport, declaring that the vibes were bad… There you go, artists are unpredictable.'

Robin Smith has also discovered the importance of not holding grudges. In 1998, he was left out of the English Test side with no reason given, even though he had just had a successful tour of South Africa. 'It's frustrating because I still have a tremendous desire to play for England,' he told *The Sunday Times*, admitting to twinges of jealousy. 'The worst thing is that nobody ever gave me a reason for dropping me at the end of that South African tour. But that was Ray Illingworth and his merry band of men.'

The *Independent on Sunday*, writing about the same episode, said: 'It is clear that Smith feels bafflement rather than rancour at being left out of the England set-up.' Smith himself says: 'I don't hold a grudge.' He had already shown this magnanimity of spirit. The previous year, the cricketer received £25,000 instead of the £205,000 profits from his benefit season. Although he gave a lot of it to charity, there was a huge discrepancy and an individual connected with the fund was investigated by the police. Smith had planned to use his benefit money as a retirement nest egg but instead, the family had to sell their 16th-century, four-bedroom house in five acres on the edge of the New Forest at Whiteparish, Wiltshire.

Smith was determined to see the positive side even in this. He told Jo Knowsley of the *Sunday Telegraph*: 'I love the game and had planned to play into my late thirties. Now it's important to do well. If things are too smooth and you have no setbacks at all, it is all too easy to sit back.'

Smith's perspective is partly shaped by his sense of his own good fortune in being healthy, with healthy children. For the past decade he has run and cycled marathons for charity after visiting a disabled boy in a home. 'What my experience with those wonderful children has taught me is that there can be no excuse for not trying to get the very best out of your ability. If I start to feel sorry for myself, one mental image of their problems soon puts a stop to it.'

Perhaps the best object lesson in dealing with failure and disappointment comes from Roger Black, whose career was dogged not only by injury but by viruses, which he says were worse. To an extent, injury is part of the toll extracted from athletes. As Black says:

> It's because what we do is just crazy. What the human body is made for, and what Olympic athletes do to it, are two different things. To be the best in the world now, you have to really push yourself to that point where you're going to go over the edge sometimes, because it you don't get close to the edge, you know you're taking up too much space. You have to get to that point or you're not going to compete any more.

When you have a broken foot, everyone sympathises because they can see you've got a problem. When you have a virus you're tired – or you don't know you have it because it hasn't been diagnosed yet – and you're training with your training partners, but you're not quite there, they're going to think you've lost it. The easiest thing to say is, 'Oh, you're mentally weak, toughen up.' It is awful because you feel pathetic, your confidence goes, your physical strength goes and that's when you really find out whether you're prepared to go right back to the start again, and fortunately I was.

The plunging morale which all of us have felt at times is no less severe when it happens to someone like Roger Black, an individual upon whom nature and nurture have shone so prodigiously. He retired suddenly, the exact date taken out of his hands, when the British selectors left him out of the squad for the European championships in Budapest in 1998.

The shock and hurt of rejection hit Black so hard that he could not speak, literally. In an interview with Kate Battersby in the *Evening Standard*, he said: 'I was devastated. I was all on my own when I got the phone call. It wasn't real. I was gobsmacked, speechless for 10 minutes. I'm never speechless. I physically couldn't speak, I was so choked. Then I got very upset and angry, and after that I hardly spoke for two days.'

Two days was all he gave himself. After that, Black knew he had to leave that episode behind and cut loose. Within a week, he was telling the Press Association:

I can walk away now knowing I've done my bit and I can move on ... Iwan [Thomas] and Mark [Richardson] have moved ahead of me and I'm going to enjoy watching them battle it out for golds and silvers for the next five or six years. One day I will be able to say I was part of that. The events of the last week will soon be a distant memory. And you know you've made the right decision when it sits with you for two days and it's not an issue.

Black had already moved on from disappointment and was putting the deselection into its place in his long and successful career.

I chose the year I was going to retire. I knew I was going to retire in 1998, but I didn't know how it was going to happen. I came fourth by two hundredths of a seconds and I felt they should have given me the selection period, two weeks, to give me a chance to get into the team. Once they had made the decision, that was it. The best thing about it was that 99 per cent of the British public were furious about it, which was nice to know.

I had to make a decision about what I was going to do from that point onwards. There was nothing more for me to do. My time had come and I was happy to retire and get on with the rest of my life. I still get people coming up to me now and getting angry about what they did. It didn't matter as much to me as I think people thought it should because I had won my Olympic medal. When I stood down from the Olympic rostrum in 1996 I absolutely remember what I said to myself: don't ever forget this, because it doesn't matter what happens from here. It won't get any better than this. I never forgot that, so I wasn't going to let one moment of not being selected make me forget that moment. So once it was on, I turned my back and that was it, off I went.

Injuries, viruses and disappointments, Black says, have held him back temporarily – then spurred him on. The following observation is perhaps the seminal truth about mistakes and failures:

Had I not been ill, I don't think I would have won an Olympic silver medal in 1996. The only reason I won that was because of all the things that had happened to me in the eight years prior to that. The injuries give you a burning desire, because you appreciate health so much more when you have been injured. I don't think I would have lasted in the sport until I was 32 if I had been healthy all the time, and in many ways I don't think I would have gone on to the career I have gone on to.

Your successes in life are what people see, but it's your failures in life, your disappointments, and how you deal with them, that shape you. The strength that's prepared me for the rest of my life is not from having medals round my neck and national anthems being played – any idiot can enjoy that. It's from being out of the sport for two years, and from the illness. In many ways it gives me a better perspective. If you win all the time, you don't have a good perspective. It has prepared me for the business world far better.

8 All that glisters...

When we are young and the world is a simple place, many of us look at successful, wealthy people and wonder why they don't buy themselves a third home by a white beach and spend the days dipping into the sea and sipping cocktails. Later, we realize that, in both life and career, fulfilment and satisfaction are not in direct proportion to the ownership of money and the ability to spend it.

We asked our subjects about money and its place in their estimation of their own success. We also asked them to summarize what success meant to them. Did it mostly mean wealth? After all, all have done well from their careers (and several have made it on to lists dedicated to winkling out the richest in the country). Did it mean influence? Are wealth and influence noticeably connected? Is it easy to get carried away with one's own self-importance and, if it is, what keeps your feet on the ground? One certainty we know – from study after study – is that money alone is not a good motivator. It rarely keeps people slogging away once they have acquired as much as they need to sustain even an affluent lifestyle. Brilliantly successful people have more complex, sophisticated needs than earning money. They desire recognition, supremacy, challenge, and they rarely consider retirement. The money is nice, but other aspects are more so. Ken Bates, estimated to be worth £50 million, and one of the 500 richest people in England, is 66 and not even contemplating giving up. Why? To him, the reason is straightforward. 'What will I do?' he asks. Those who have brilliant careers live and breathe them. They don't do what they do merely to earn a living. They do it because they love it. On the few occasions that retirement has crossed Bates's mind – fleetingly – one image can dispel it:

> When I was in Lancashire I used to see these people who'd go down for their holidays and fall in love with Torquay on a nice sunny day. They all go there to retire and live there and walk up and down looking at other miserable old people and moaning all day. I never quite understood why you spent your life building up a network of friends – and I believe I've done that – and seeing interesting places…[and then give it up]. Surely it makes sense to do what you enjoy doing for the rest of your life. Perhaps maybe holiday more…

Is money a motivator? Bates says: 'If you do something properly and do it well, then the money will follow. But if you're out there to make money only, you might succeed, but you'll be pretty miserable. You're better doing something well. The art of perfection is an interesting one.' How does this transfer to football, where players demand (and receive) fortunes during their playing career? Bates says:

> Football is still basically a sport [rather than a business] because if you don't play well, people won't come and watch you. Now you have international players earning extremely large salaries, then it has to run as a business. But heaven forbid that we ever get to the stage where supporters and players cannot cavort on the pitch after they've won the Cup or the champions' league.

Money and sport are a volatile mix. When Sebastian Coe went for an interview as national middle-distance coach for Switzerland, he damaged his chances when he said that too much state money was being given to athletes for merely getting into the national side, which robbed them of motivation. When he added that he would also take away their sponsored cars, the Swiss could not show him the door fast enough! Robin Smith concurs that too much too soon can tend to shift the focus of sportsmen away from the game and towards a desirable lifestyle.

If one asks successful people about what their success means to them, the responses are totally unpredictable (sometimes even poetic!). No one ever says – honestly – that it's about being rich. The belief that money has motivated them to do well can be galling. No one writes about Nicola Horlick without mention of her salary, her house and her lifestyle, but her responses to questions about achieve ment are much more complex. For her, becoming successful was more about escape from a more painful life at home: the knowledge that her eldest child might not survive.

> I've tried to say that all that [wealth and possessions] is irrelevant. My experience in life, particularly the experience of having a very sick child who subsequently died, has been that all of that is actually completely irrelevant. I'm not living in poverty, I can say that. Nonetheless, I think people think it's all about that – that the reason I've worked is so that I can have a Mercedes or a nice house, but it isn't. In fact, in many ways it's been a form of escape.
>
> What a lot of people don't realize is that Georgie, my daughter, who had leukaemia, was actually diagnosed when she was two, and she died when she was 12. So we had a long period of time battling against a very serious disease. I can't say, in all honesty, with my hand on my heart, that I would necessarily have worked if I hadn't been in that situation. In a way, it was a form of escape from the horror of it all. I found that when I was at home by myself or with just one or two children that I would dwell on it an awful lot, and I sort of needed work to help me take my mind off it.

Success to Horlick is 'not power'. She says: 'I get a kick out of watching others succeed. There are people around the City now running businesses who were once my graduate trainees. I am really pleased that I trained them; I think I trained them well and now they've gone on to be very successful.' Horlick explored achievement in her book, *Can You Have It All?*, and concluded that the answer to that question was clearly 'no'.

> The Mercedes car, the house – these are what some people seem to think are important, and I thought that too, maybe, when I was in my twen-ties. But from the very moment Georgie was diagnosed as having

leukaemia, my life changed forever. I had to live with that for a very long period of time and now I have to live with the fact that I am never going to see her again. How can all these things be important in the context of that? Certainly you can't have it all. No one can have it all. It's a cruel place.

The pleasure of success is not usually a solitary affair. When things are going well for Tony Bullimore, his thoughts wander: to the pleasure his success will give to his sponsors.

My greatest thrill was to be made Yachtsman of the Year in 1985, when I won 28 races throughout Europe. It wasn't the title: it was the fact that I had done the right things to achieve it… There is nothing finer than when my project is roaring along and we're not only getting a return [for the sponsor] but the return is well in excess of what people expected. I've had the chairmen of very large organizations actually fly down to the Mediterranean and come to a reception just to see us receive the trophy.

Bullimore has enough money, and enough is all he wants. Having worked out what brings him pure joy, he wants to be able to carry on doing it.

Many years ago I was interested in acquiring a lot of money. I wanted to be very successful in business, I wanted a lot of money, and then I would have reached my Shangri-La. As the years have rolled by, I've got older and I'm all right – nowhere near that kind of league, but it doesn't worry me. Now I would like to have a comfortable life. I'd like to do the things I'm doing, to continue racing for another three or four years. I want to race round the world another three times, and I've got one or two other little projects up my sleeve.

The event that shot Bullimore to such fame, of course, also cost the Australians millions of dollars for the rescue mission. Helicopters had to be scrambled quickly, a crew for the boat, people were virtually being dragged out of pubs and homes to crew both. Bullimore felt a twinge of guilt, but the Australians were quick to tell him to banish it.

Although there were one of two people in Australia and other parts of the world who asked who was going to pay the millions of dollars it had cost to do all this, I was told by a senior member of the Australian information services, 'Don't be embarrassed about what happened. We spend millions of dollars all over the world through our high commissions and embassies and other agencies promoting Australia for inward investment and exports. We can never really gauge how well we do. One thing is for sure: the few million dollars we spent on rescuing you has given us more positive promotion, public relations, goodwill and global awareness of what Australia is about.' Everyone felt a great feeling of wellbeing, and they still do, towards Australia and the Australian people for what they did. They didn't have to do it, but they did.

Chay Blyth, our other brilliant yachtsman, has made a thriving business out of sailing. Yet he keeps going – well into his sixties – not to amass a bigger stash, but to keep tapping into the euphoria of those who take part in his BT Global Challenge. He looks at them, and he sees himself.

The BT Global Challenge is about people seeing beyond their natural horizons. It is about the spirit that makes someone ignore seasickness and lack of sleep, pull on a damp set of thermals and struggle on deck at 3 am to make a sail change. That says more about you than any status symbol.

Blyth's nightmare is not to die only moderately wealthy, but to regret what he never did.

One day, you're going to lie in your bed and look at your toes. And you'll ask yourself a question in the quiet of the night: have I enjoyed life, have I done all I wanted to do? If the answer's no, you're going to be really pissed off! I think that in the dead of the night I'm going to look at my toes and think, well we did make a fortune – and Christ, we did have a few laughs.

The bulk of the reason [for running the business] is not profit, although it helps. The main reason is that I can identify very clearly with the people. I interview every single person who goes in the race, personally and face-to-face, with the exception of one or two because of distance or time. I don't offer a berth to about 20 per cent and I identify very clearly with them because the money is £24,850, a huge sum, spread over four years. It's exactly as I was when I wanted to go round the world as well, because I couldn't get sponsorship, I had to sell my house, my wife had to go out to work when we had a small child and a mortgage. I had a good career with Schweppes. So I know the difficulties they have to raise that money. Equally, it's an opportunity for them because it's a springboard, potentially, to something else. It's an opportunity as well as an adventure and a challenge.

This is how Blyth views his own success:

It depends what your needs are. If you want big cars, big houses and things like that, that will manifest itself as your success. In my case it's fairly small things. I like dealing with people, I like being with young people, it's all to do with just enjoying your life. That's a factor in all the things you've done. No matter how big you are, how important you might think you are, you'll make very little impression in this life. I'm laid back. If the whole thing collapsed tomorrow, we'd just say well, it's a bit of a duff thing, think of another thing to do. [For me] success is not measured in big things. It's just being generally content.

Wealth is something Michael Parkinson never thought to achieve back in south Yorkshire. The influence of his secure, working-class background has remained with him. When he imagines himself under pressure, he thinks of his father. As he told *The Sunday Times* in January 1998, before his return to the screen: 'People talk about pressure today. Pressure? My father had to be up at four. You didn't get paid till you reached the seam. You'd been walking for three bloody hours before you got there.'

Success to Parkinson means 'not having to worry':

You're bound inevitably to measure success in terms of achieving what you want to be. I don't want to be the richest man in the world, but I don't want to be the poorest either. I want to come to the point in my life where I don't have to worry about anybody around me in terms of finances. That's success in my book, coming from where I come from. The chances of that happening were fairly unlikely. But the greatest success is never actually having been bored in the job I do and getting up every morning and thinking 'this is rather pleasant, I have to go to work this morning'. I can't imagine my father woke up too often and thought 'I'm overjoyed at the prospect of going to work at Grimethorpe Colliery'. That's success – that I never had to face that.

If wealth is not a major motivator in a brilliant career, could it actually act as a disincentive? Two of our subjects think that the dominance of money in their fields has blunted competitive edges. A third – Michael Lynagh – fears it will, to some extent, curb the characters of his game. A fourth – Harvey Goldsmith – laments 'a whole industry' of money men who have dispelled the magic inherent in the business.

I'm actually very fussy, and if I don't enjoy a particular sort of entertainment, I can't put my heart into it, even if I know it's going to make a lot of money. If most artists had their way, all tickets would be £10…what's happened is that the industry has grown up with a whole slew of lawyers, accountants, business advisers, bankers, all sorts of people, all of whom have their hand in the till. I think it's terribly sad, and has perverted what artists really want to do. Most of them say, 'Listen, I'm going out to earn some money – if you want to come and see me, great, and if you don't, that's also great.' It isn't so much a protection of the artists' money and their rights, which is the natural way of doing things – it's become the protection of all those people around it, to try to justify themselves. So a whole industry has sprung up around our business and on too many occasions the business side is driving the creativity, and it is terribly wrong.

Of all his career achievements, Goldsmith counts Live Aid as the one that gave him the most personal satisfaction. It not only raised £140 million but showed, he says, 'that long-haired drug-crazed hippies can do good in the world, showing the pathway forward'. Pavarotti in the Park was another surreal and wonderful experience that transcended the ordinary:

> It poured down with rain, and somewhere in the region of 120,000 to 150,000 people had this extraordinary experience of a great tenor playing with a great orchestra, playing on stage while it's bucketing down with rain. On the front row, with plastic sheets over them, was the Prime Minister, three-quarters of the Cabinet, the Prince and Princess of Wales, joining in the fun.

Greed – on the part of professional advisers rather than artists – destroys the magic of music, Goldsmith says. The key to success is keeping up demand; demand only exists when it exceeds supply: 'My whole ethos of business is that if you can sell 11,000 seats, play a 10,000-seater. What's happened today is that we've lost that demand value. If you can't get a ticket, as everyone knows, everybody wants one.' Goldsmith tried out his theory with Bob Dylan and Santana at Wembley Stadium. Tickets were selling slowly and he was wondering whether to do more advertising. Instead, he decided to enhance demand by withdrawing all tickets apart from 20 pairs in each box office.

> In two weeks we went from 36,000 to 71,000 tickets. The box offices were saying they'd only got five tickets left, and the customers were saying, 'We'll buy them now.' The important factor is keeping this demand up, and what the industry is doing is exhausting that demand, pushing records from the record industry as far as they possibly can, until nobody wants to buy one, instead of saving some for the next album. With ticket sales, if you can play 11,000 seats [the ethos is] try 15,000 seats – you never know, you might make another £100,000 – and by the way, Mr Promoter, could you pay us on the basis of 15,000 seats as you know, really, that you can play 15,000. Because if you don't do it, you'd only lose money on it and destroy the artist's career. Artists are based on dreams, heroism, the myth and magic of going on stage – they're absolutely based on demand.

Robin Smith has never pursued money despite some 'unbelievable offers' from other counties. 'It makes you feel really good about yourself – at least there's somebody out there who needs your services – but I would never use that to go to the club and say I could get x amount more at another club. As long as the club appreciates that and appreciates my loyalty, and I continue at Hampshire for a few more years, I'll be happy.' Smith says he feels a sense of loyalty to the club that has supported him throughout his career:

> I don't want to sound arrogant, because I certainly hope I'm not. I have had an enormous number of offers to go and play elsewhere but Hampshire has always been very good to me. When I came over as a 17-year-old they offered me a four-year contract and I have never had to renegotiate my contract. They have always paid me money I'm quite happy with, although players are getting paid a lot more elsewhere. As long as I'm happy, I've always been one of those people who doesn't worry about others. If their negotiating powers are better than mine – if there's a bloke at Hampshire not half as good as I am getting more than half as much money – I don't mind. It's up to me to go and negotiate my own contract. If he's negotiated more than me, good luck to him. I do feel a sense of loyalty. I love Hampshire, I have a lot of friends there, I have been very well supported. I would always like to continue playing for Hampshire.

Smith says that too much too soon takes away ambition and desire:

> I don't know whether the youngsters from a cricketing point of view get things too easily. I can't pinpoint the problem, but even in Hampshire, they come into the side, they have lovely apartments down at Ocean Village, they go out every night, they have a great quality of life, sponsored cars, good bonuses, lovely clothes. I sometimes wonder whether it does come a little bit too easy for them and they don't work hard enough for the great pleasures in life they get, especially so early in their careers. I would never criticize that as long as they put in the hard work and appreciate what they have and are grateful – but people in this country seem to have an easier life than those brought up the hard way in the sub-continents.

Big bucks swimming around sport, Smith says, foster desperate measures.

> The emphasis on winning cricket matches is bigger because without winning we don't get our major sponsors. Channel Four has just pumped £104 million into English cricket and there is an enormous amount at stake. We have to perform. With that comes a lot of frustration when things aren't going our way, and with that comes sledging. I do feel the umpires should have the authority at the end of the game to fine players, and make sure it's a worthwhile fine.

Michael Lynagh believes that rugby players should be paid, but says Australian rugby staggered briefly when the game first turned professional.

> I remember in 1985 the atmosphere changed quite a bit around World Cup time. That word 'money' started to arrive. It was the first time that Australian rugby players were offered contracts if they made the squad. There was about 30 of us going to the World Cup and I had a feeling that there were some young guys on that trip who were content just to make the squad, they weren't really interested in contributing to our success or to our failure. In fact it was all a bit much, and they stood back from it and didn't want to inject themselves because of the fear of failure. I'm pleased to say that that has changed now in Australian rugby, but there was a real atmosphere for a while. Actually, one of the reasons I decided to retire in 1995 was because of that, things were changing.

Given a choice between a seat in Parliament and an Olympic medal, Sebastian Coe would choose the medal. He has never pursued wealth and holds strong views about the place of money, and says there is a delicate balance in funding athletes – too much can be demotivating. When he met the Swiss to talk about becoming their national middle-distance coach, he was already familiar with the set-up because his father had coached a runner who finished sixth in the Olympic 1500 metres (behind Coe) in 1984.

We looked at the situation quite closely, and one of the things we felt was actually demotivating was that some of the athletes were getting far too much state support. They only had to get into their team to get a sponsored car or an apartment. If we are being brutal about it, they were a bit soft. I remember the first question I got asked was what would I do to improve this. I said I would remove all the state funding and take all the sponsored cars away. The interview didn't last very long! That is a very general response. I don't want to see lottery funding just handed out to anybody that thinks they have got a particularly good case. It has got to be aspirational and inspirational.

I want to see the funding targeted and I want to see it really being used to maximum effect. It is state funding and I think there is a responsibility for the governing body of that sport to say, 'You have a responsibility to prepare properly and be in shape for major championships.' That shop window is going to encourage others into your sport. Squandering that talent all over the place in races that are not remotely helpful to an Olympic championship or a world championship should be controlled as well. I think there is a lot that should go with lottery funding [in the way of] what governing bodies expect out of their competitors once they have received the money.

Coe's view of his own success is that it did not come with money or recognition; there is no specific point at which success is gained: 'This is a cliché, but I think it is true all the same. Success is not a product; it is a process. Success can come at so many different levels, but actually success is about the lifestyle you choose.'

Michael Lynagh describes his own success in terms of great moments on the field; great characters he has been able to play against and alongside, and his best-ever moment: winning the World Cup quarter-final against Ireland in 1991 by planning and executing a strategy under extreme pressure (Ireland were leading by three points with four minutes to go).

Celebrity, though … now there's an interesting phenomenon. What happens when you start (as they say) to believe your own publicity, as surely you must? 'I've always been immune [to the glitz of showbiz],' says Harvey Goldsmith, who has been surrounded by it all his working life.

I look on it as part of my work; rarely do I think of the glamour. To us it's just a job. We're really dealing with the other side of it, keeping people away or pushing people forward. We're never quite on the side where we can step back and enjoy it, unless I'm going to somebody else's event.

Michael Parkinson says he was old enough, at 35, to handle fame and keep it in perspective. 'I know it's just a job, and I've devised a way of doing it. I'm proud of it, but I don't think I'm anything special. It ain't no big deal. I'm just a hack working away in a strange business,' he says. Remembering his place – not the star of the show – has enabled him to remain consummately skilled at his job. He studied his craft by watching John Freeman, one of the first TV interviewers, and noticed that he was hardly seen, only heard.

John Freeman became the most famous man on television and you didn't see him. You only actually heard him ask a question. The camera was locked on to the face of the person he was talking to. I thought there was a lesson there: that the interviewer is the person, the means, by which the public asks the question. Inevitably there comes a point where you become famous. It happens to all of us actually, where you begin to think that you're a competitor, rather than an interviewer, but generally speaking, you have got to keep that down. You're doing a job.

Parkinson feels for those who have been, and who continue to be, bowled over by the whirlwind of fame. George Best, he says, suffered because there was no one there to keep him grounded.

There was no infrastructure around George at all. He was the first one and bigger than any of them. You never saw anybody as glamorous as George. He'd got big violet eyes and lashes that were eight feet long, he was this thin, and he played football like a genius. He was the most extraordinary creature you had ever seen, but it came at the time when there was no infrastructure or protection around him.

At least the kids nowadays have got half a chance – except that when you look at the people around them, you begin to worry; so-called agents and people like that. You also worry about the lack of care there is in football clubs. They are only interested in the commodity, not the whole person. I feel sorry for kids like that, who are growing up in this extraordinary world, this goldfish bowl. I had it easy, I was 35, married with three kids, when it came to me. I'm from Yorkshire too, for Christ's sake. I'm probably going to get more aggressive, more belligerent, more opinionated, but I'm not going to do silly things.

Parkinson's feet were kept on *terra firma* by his father, among others:

My dad always thought I was a failure for two reasons. One was because I had never interviewed Alice Faye or Betty Grable, who were his two great sex symbols. I let him down badly. Worst of all, he said to me about a year before he died, 'You've had a good time, haven't you?' I said, 'Yes, I have, I've been very lucky.' He said, 'Yeah, you've made some money,' and I said, 'I'm all right, dad.' He said, 'You've met all them birds.' I said, 'I did, Ingrid Bergman, and all that.' He said, 'And you're famous.' I said, 'I am.' Then he said, 'Think on. It's not like playing [cricket] for Yorkshire.' I just thought, that'll probably go on my tombstone. The way he was defining it, that was the difference between fame and immortality. Being famous is easy by comparison.

Tony Bullimore resists the temptation to accept other people's assessment that his survival was heroic and he is, therefore, a bit of a hero.

I think that, quite frankly, is a bit embarrassing. The real heroes were the Australian defence forces: the Navy, the Air Force, the rescue services, the people who put themselves out and really tried. The people who left *The Adelaide* and crossed in a little rubber boat in really dodgy seas to see whether I was under the boat – they are the people who put it together.

Chay Blyth has been said by the *Glasgow Herald* to have 'done more than anyone to demystify and debunk yachting's élitist image'. Knighted in 1997 for 'services to sailing', he said it was 'fantastic for a boy from the factory floor to go all the way to being knighted, but I'm still the same ordinary guy. I queue up in the chip shop like I always did.'

Furthermore, Blyth is Scottish. The Scots have their own ways.

I come from a small town in Scotland, Hawick, and they're a total outfit unto their own. They're not impressed by me at all, principally because I don't play rugby – and if you don't play rugby in Hawick, you're a poofter! It's quite good. I'm certainly kept on the floor there.

I'm also a freeman of the borough. I've just come back from six weeks up there, where we have a local festival with a big event in the town hall. I said to the chairman, 'Is it possible to have two tickets?' and he said 'Oh, we haven't got two tickets for you!' I've got the only knighthood in the town and am the only freeman of the borough and there's no way they'll get me on an official platform. I try to keep myself firmly on the floor. I stop at these wayside caravans and have a sandwich and a cup of tea. It's easy enough to stop off at a hotel but you stand there with the truckers and have a few words with them and they don't know you from Adam.

Sebastian Coe spent little time in the ether surrounding top-class athletes: he moved straight to the business of politics, where he was a victim of the Conservative defeat after only five years. The problems of his constituency kept him grounded.

I got into areas which in the past had been slightly no-go areas for traditional Conservative candidates. That's something I was pleased and proud about. The one thing that people forget about Cornwall is that for most people it's a holiday destination. Cornwall is actually an area of acute deprivation in some areas. I represented a constituency in the Redruth-Camborne area, which was effectively the remnants of the old tin-mining industry and the engineering industry. I had miners' cottages that would change hands for £27,000 at one end and on the south end of my constituency I had houses that changed hands for a million and a half. There was a massive range of income spread and high levels of unemployment. An average industrial wage in Cornwall, when I left a couple of years ago, was only about £11,500–£12,000. You're talking about a population that is effectively surviving on about 75 per cent of the average industrial wage in this country. One thing I like to feel I managed to do was to keep open Europe's last remaining tin mine, which was in my constituency, five years longer than realistically it should have been. It kept 270 people in jobs.

9 Upsides and downsides

Nothing is perfect...

Media intrusion is difficult to live with. I thought it would be 15 minutes of fame, which is what most people talk about, but it seemed to go on and on. I suppose there is a high degree of sexism involved there. Being a woman had something to do with it because you don't get men in business being referred to as the father of four or five children. If you're a woman it seems to be terribly relevant to every single article, whatever it is about, that you're a mother of five children. I really wish I was an anonymous person again. All this dissection about whether [being a working mother of five] is the right thing to do...

Nicola Horlick

You encounter problems as captain of a county – the Fleet Street journalists, not only in cricket but in all sport and business as well, write you up and all of a sudden just knock you down. I'm not sure I'm into that any more. To go and captain England, I wouldn't spend any time at home at all. I went home this evening and my children had just come back from school and I had to reintroduce myself – they don't know who their daddy is any more!

Robin Smith

The problem for most child actors is that you don't really get an adolescence, you leap straight from childhood into an assumed adulthood. You are in such an adult environment. There are subliminal demands on you to be sophisticated and to be terribly disciplined. One thing about a normal adolescence is that it's a time when you can learn about being floppy. In a working environment we were never allowed to be. The biggest problem for most child actors is how to unpick that assumed adulthood and find a way to develop a real adolescence and a real adulthood. An awful lot of the people I worked with as a child ended up at worse having breakdowns or at best having sad little jobs associated with show business but not really quite being show business. There was a feeling that the real high point of their lives was when they were 12 or 13.

Tony Robinson

If I made a mistake, it was waiting until quite late in my life to go on such a major course [a six-month residential course at the London Business School]. I should have really done it when I was younger, because I found it really exciting, really tremendous.

Sir Chay Blyth, whose regrets do not include being given a lower-ranking British Empire Medal than Capt John Ridgeway (CBE) after both had rowed the Atlantic, because the system dictated different honours for different ranks.

I actually don't mind [being pestered by autograph hunters] too often... They come this close to you and back you around the room... Most people are pretty nice about it. There are not a lot of downsides.

Michael Lynagh

The British don't quite understand passion. They put it into the category of workaholism, which means somebody who is controlled by work, and who has no choice. I have made a choice, and that choice has a very strong implication in that it robs me of part of the life I would love to have: the ability to pick up wild flowers, the ability to welcome my friends in my home and look after them, the ability to see my sons more often and go to the theatre or the opera house or ballet once a week. I miss all that, but you make your choice. It is not workaholism, it is complete passion. You cannot have it all. You cannot have a great professional life and a great private life. Out of the two my private life is the more disastrous.

Raymond Blanc, whose other irritation is the food critic. ('Most of today's food critics are very vain, with egos even bigger than the chefs.')

I would have loved to have walked out at Lords and made a century for England. Would I have changed that for what I've done now? I doubt it. There was a point in my life, when I was 21, 22, when I was offered a job by Hampshire cricket club. I sometimes think now, had I gone on to be a professional cricketer, I would have been a very ordinary one. I would probably now have retired from a job as a newsagent in Southampton.

Michael Parkinson, who used to open for Barnsley with Dickie Bird and who once kept Geoffrey Boycott out of the team (when Boycott was 13).

The one thing that's been most difficult is striking the balance between razzamatazz and glamour – being in some of the most peculiar places, meeting kings, queens and princes, being let loose in the White House – and having a wife, son and family; a personal life as well. Also, maintaining friends I grew up with and others I'd like to see socially, developing the best that I can with friends who can tolerate me. With travelling, I need that balance. In order to be a complete maniac, you need basic security behind you.

Harvey Goldsmith, who adds that it is easy to make mistakes where there are still no rules, no training and no courses

You can't change it [his public image of ruthlessness], you just have to get on and live with it. The image itself doesn't really matter, it's who you are that counts. Susannah says I'm a cuddly teddy bear. You pay your penny and take your chance. The media respect me, but quite a few of them don't like me. It's a funny world generally, just like politics. When was the last time a politician gave a straight answer to a question? Never, and unfortunately that applies to football as well.

Ken Bates

I won two silvers at 800 metres but I didn't win the ultimate. Yes I would have loved to have won the Olympic title but I am not somebody who sits back and thinks what might have happened. It is probably one of my failings that I move on quite quickly. I never go back. I was very lucky. You asked me one of my proudest things and that was actually being a part of probably the greatest era in British athletics.

Sebastian Coe

I have only one regret, although lots of things I would do differently – I would get medical advice very early on in my career. I didn't achieve what I could have done because of physical injury. My regret is that I had one chance in my whole career to stand up in my own right and be champion of the world in the 1991 World Championships. I came second in the 400 metres by about this much. I should have won, I was more than capable, but I ran a reactive race. I was in phenomenal physical shape and I panicked. I hadn't learnt about running my perfect race and I never got that chance again, never.

Roger Black

...it may, however, be as near as dammit

Jeff Grout: 'Any regrets looking back over your career?'
Roger Black: 'No. None at all really.'
Jeff Grout: 'What does success mean to you?'
Roger Black: 'I am fortunate, very fortunate.'
Jeff Grout: 'Do you get pestered in restaurants?'
Roger Black: 'I get tables in restaurants.'
Jeff Grout: 'Is there a downside to being Roger Black?'
Roger Black: 'No. When you hear people saying it's awful being a celebrity, it's awful being hounded – I don't get that. Is there a downside to it? No, there isn't, really – you could find one if you wanted to, but you would have to be so detached from reality. Most of my friends have normal jobs and work very hard and would love to be me. So I'm being truthful – it's great.'

Jeff Grout: 'Is there a price to pay?'
Michael Parkinson: 'I don't think there is a price to pay. If you get success as a mature man, which I did – semi-mature; I was 35 – you have a chance.'

Tony Bullimore: 'What more can I really ask for? I've raced all the oceans, I've won 150 trophies, I've done 250,000 miles at sea. I have had a good life, I am healthy, my wife is healthy and happy and I have got a terrific project on the go at the moment, and I'm going to go for it. What more could I really ask for?'

Not that brilliant, thanks

We are happy to make clear that, despite the impression that might have been inadvertently given by a profile in the *Sunday Telegraph Magazine* of Dec 14, Mr Parkinson has never claimed that he is 'the best bloody interviewer in the world'.

Sunday Telegraph, December 1997

Index